MONUMENTAL

Monumental

It Was Never About A Statue

authored by

Dr. Wes Bellamy

For My Wife and Baby Girls,
You Mean the World to Me

Table of Contents

Acknowledgement

I would like to first give honor to my Lord and Savior Jesus Christ. Thank you, Lord for never leaving me, never forsaking me, and guiding me through this process.

I would next like to thank my wife, Ashlee Bellamy, for sticking with me throughout this process. It has been a journey for sure, and I am extremely appreciative for you. This book is yours as much as it is mine. You've stuck with me during the craziest time of my life all while having to adjust to being in a foreign land with different cultures and stepping out of your comfort zone. You did it all with grace, class, and the beauty of the woman that I've fallen in love with three times over.

To my daughters, Laila, Makaylah, and Londyn: Thank you for being my motivation. Baby girls, I know it hasn't been easy. Dad has to travel a lot, dad gets stopped all of the time when we are out, and I'm usually very hard on you all. Just know that you three mean more to me than anything else in the world. I sacrifice daily so that you can have whatever you need whenever you need it. Love you. All of this is for you all.

Thank you to my Aunt Delaphine Crosland for saving my life, and thank you to my mother Jacqueline Joyce and my father Windale Bellamy for giving me life. I'm glad that our relationships have grown into what they are today. You all did the best that you could. I'm not upset at all, you made me who I am. Love ya'll. To my stepfather Prince Joyce, thank you for everything. Glad we have grown into what we are today. To my little brother Javin, I love you. You were the first person to show me that my words matter. I'm more proud of you than you will ever know. I love you. I wish I could explain the love I have for you in words, but I can't. Just know that you're my world little man! Finish that degree! Rest in power to my grandmother Evie Mae Bellamy, my Great Grandmother MeMe and my Aunt Margaret Windley, and Uncle Vernon. My cousins, Tiffany and Stephany and Alquen, love you forever. I know I terrorized y'all as a kid, but it was all worth it. My big brothers, Eric and Leon thanks for being a lifeline and saving me. Thanks for always being there for me. To Shateria, Shahaddah, Anandai, Ina, Timmy, Rickey, Chris, and your children, I love you. To my first hero, Lucus Green, thanks for being a role model. My Uncle George Windley SR., Thank you for saving my life. God sent you to me when I needed you most. My cousin George JR. Thanks for being my older brother. Thanks for believing in me from the start. Jeremiah 1:1-8.

Much love to my family in SC and Atlanta!

To my mentor Dr. L. Bernard Hairston, thank you for being my educational father and role model. Almost everything that I do is to make you proud and to live up to your legacy. Thank you for being so hard on me, holding me accountable, but also believing in me and allowing me to grow into my own man. Thank you Ms. Pearl Early for being my educational mother. I honestly don't know where I would be without you. I love you

To my brothers Hodari, Quinton, Waki, Will, Matt Murphy and Damani thank you for saving my life. My brothers Khalil, Nathaniel, and Verne, DBC for Life. Love y'all forever. Thank you for keeping me sane. Thank you for allowing me to be myself. Love y'all. To the brothers at His Image Barbershop, Ray, Jamal, Bear, and RC) thank y'all for allowing me to be myself and not a character. Thank you for allowing me to just come in and be a regular person. Love y'all more than you ever know.

To my brothers Rusty, DJ, Kwame, and Corey thank you for being my accountability partners. We push each other to be better daily. Love y'all.

To my brothers Big Shot, Barry, Bo, Tooda, Ron, and Malik, thanks for believing in me from the beginning. Thanks for taking me under your wing and helping me grow. My wife's family. Thank you for keeping us in prayer and holding us down. Levon, Dominique, Jarrahd, Rest In Power Aunt Hattie, thanks Uncle Horrace. Love you Monica and Tron, Poppa Harry Jr., Aunt Shirley, Uncle Luther, Brittany, Kionna, Chell, Mrs. Tanyah, Ashlynne, Matt, Anthony, Sammy, and all of her friends and family in Charlottesville, Columbia, Orangeburg, and elsewhere, Thank you for loving my wife. Thank you watching over her, and being there for her when she needed someone to talk to. Personally, it means a lot!

To my Family in the Movement:
To my sisters Symone Sanders, Angela Rye, Alicia Garza, Lea Webb Shemica Bowen, Mimi B., Traci DeShazor, Jennifer Bowles, Stephanie Morales, Adjoa, Temi Bennet, Tami Sawyer, Dr. Erica Southerland, Tanyah Barnes, LaSharece Aird, Alexis Rodgers, AND EVERYONE ELSE Thank you!

To my brothers, Jewell Jones, Rev. Stephen Green, Carlos Moore, Joe Dillard JR., Tyrell Holcomb, Markus Batchelor, Brandon Scott, Taikeen Cooper, Van Jones, David Bowen, Ariel Guerrero, Kevin Carter, Johnathan Randle, and EVERYONE ELSE! Love you. Lieutenant Governor Justin Fairfax, John Chapman

South Carolina State Fam: Trustee Hamilton Grant, Congressman Jim Clyburn, Bryanta Maxwell, Dr. Ora Spann, David White JR., the whole 300, JA, BoCat, Big Juice, Blu, Noc, Avery, Keem, Marvis, Ty, 22 BONDS, for real the entire school! I appreciate the life lessons.

All of my students at Virginia State University and Virginia Union University, I love you. I expect nothing short of greatness from you because we operate in excellence. You are the chosen ones to lead the next generation! Like we always say in class, "Let's think critically, find the solution, and then move to the next!" Be better than Dr. B. If I can you can, and you have a head start!

I would also like to extend my deep appreciation and gratitude to the City of Charlottesville, Virginia. Y'all grew me up. Took me from a crazy young man that knew everything to a husband, father, and better man. I love you forever. Serving as your Vice Mayor while earning my doctoral degree and writing my dissertation was one of the toughest things that I have ever had to do. Serving you in general had been a pleasure. This entire last few year has been the craziest of my life, but the city of Charlottesville has always had my back. The people of our city encouraged me to no end. While I was down, when I felt like quitting, and when I felt like moving to somewhere else where life would be easier, it is the city of Charlottesville that reminded me of my purpose. I am forever grateful to all of you for pushing me to be a better scholar, a better elected official, and most importantly, a better man. To my friends and family, everyone who asked me over and over "Aren't you finished with that thing yet?" Everyone who prayed for me, kept me in your thoughts and sent me positive energy, thank you. To my pastors, Hodari Hamilton, Rev. Dr. Earl Pendleton, and Rev. Dr. Alvin Edwards, thank you. I could not have done any of this without your divine encouragement. I am forever grateful to Dr. Linda Noel Batiste. I will never forget our first encounter during the first year of my Master's program in 2013, and you yelled at me like I was your son. I thought you were going to make my life Hell on Earth, but in all actuality, you have been an angel in disguise. Thank you for holding me accountable to no end.

Thank you for believing in me.

Waaaaaaaayyy too many to name but I'm going to take a shot:

Much love to #NEWCville: My ride or die, fighting whoever for me whenever and then we going to fight each other lol Tanesha Hudson. You really get on my last nerve, like the last one! But you always got my back. Appreciate that.

My Mayor, Nikuyah Walker. Thank you for sacrificing your time, energy, and mental for me when they were trying to take everything from me. Thanks for challenging me to think harder. You get on my nerves sometimes too, but I love you sis.

My oldest baby girl Zy Bryant, all I can do is shake my head lol. Sometimes I wish we never would have spoken about this statue stuff lol. But seriously, watching you grow has been one of the highlights of my life. I love you like my own. I know I'm hard on you in the texts, I know I'm always pushing you, we don't agree on everything, but I'm incredibly proud of you and the leadership you've developed through all of this. You have challenged me, pushed me, and we've grown together.
Love you.

Lisa Green, Amy Sarah Marshall and all of Cville Pride, thanks for having my back! Love y'all. Yolunda Coles-Jones, Yolanda Harrell, Tracy Wynn, thank you for being there for my family. Tanisha Thompson, my sister. I love you. You've been a mother, an aunt, sister, and everything else. I can never repay you, but I'm appreciative. Joy Johnson, Deidra Gilmore, Shymora Cooper, Melvin Burress, Mayor Dave Norris, Mark Brown, John Kluge, Christie Mahoney, Audrey Oliver, Latia Tolbert, Snake, Swamp, Corbin, BallHawk, Dixon, Kofi, Gooch,Steve, Chris, Big Sharp, Buck from 1st St., Dean - Face, Charles Lewis, Dan Fairley, the 100, Momma Leah P., Mimi Mitsziko, Big CJ, Eric Johnson, JD, Marcia, Sharon, Tamara, Uncle Fuss Linden, my brother Tony Lucadamo, Uncle James Bryant, Chief Al Thomas, Dr. Andrea Douglas, Dr. Jalane Schmidt, Jane Smith, Dr. Bob

Guest, Dr. M. Rick Turner, Jimmy Hollins and Burley Varsity Club, Dr. Marcus Martin, Andrea Copeland-Whitset and Bernard Whitset, Louisa Jeanette, Robert Gray, Will Isabella, Jamar Pierre-Louis, Courtney Commander, Brandon and Christie Isaiah, Leilani Keys, Rev. Brenda Brown-Grooms, Frank Duke, Jim Hengely, Ron Tweel, Andrew Sneathern, Lawton Tuffs, Governor McAuliffe, Governor Northam, Alumni Chapter of Kappa Alpha Psi, African American Teaching Fellows, ACPS, CCS, and **THE WHOLE CITY!**

A Special thanks to Kristin Szakos. We started this journey together and it was tough. At times we didn't know if we would make it. We laughed together, cried together, stood tall together, and defended each other. Thank you for being a friend. Love you forever.

And last but not least:

Thank you to everyone who sent me a tweet, an Instagram message, email, and/or Facebook message, in person conversation, prayer from afar, and word of encouragement. Finally, thank you to the ancestors and everyone whose shoulders that I am standing on. I am forever grateful for everyone who sacrificed their bodies, their minds, and their spirits for us to be here today. I vow to make you proud.

This book is not my own....
This is OURS!

Preface

   In the shadows, in the valleys where people often didn't look, there was a group of people who were watching. Around our blue dot community of Charlottesville, Virginia, there was a sea of red who believed Black Lives Matter was a terrorist organization and that Blacks were making too much noise. These shadows believed that they were losing power and influence as people of color rose up, that "their" city was changing, and not for the better. The 27-Year-Old outspoken Vice Mayor, was also a loud mouth Black Supremacist who only stirred things up, and they were determined to show him that they would do whatever it took to Make America (and Charlottesville) Great Again.

"I looked death in the face years back, I held tears back, I gathered myself and stared back."

This Jay-Z line played in my head over and over on this brisk morning in March of 2016 as I looked at 100 people yelling at me, calling me every name imaginable, and literally wishing death on me for merely suggesting at a press conference that the statue of Robert E. Lee should be moved out of the public park in the middle of our city.

Some warned me, but in my naivety, I believed that things were different. It was a new day, a new era, and the Robert E. Lee statue needed to be moved, because it didn't represent our city's values. Naturally, everyone would agree. I soon learned that I was wrong. Some would not only disagree, they would kill to prove that they were right.

They came with torches, they came with swords and shields, they came with guns. They came with signs that called me the N-Word, they tried to take my livelihood, break down my family, and send us all a message. It was deeper than a statue. My city was in the midst of a change that the world would see. This monumental shift would have ramifications felt across the world, and through my eyes, it was a fight that almost cost me everything, but it was all worth it. Step into my shoes and read what it felt like to be in the midst of a war for the soul of our community.

The removal of a statue is one thing, but this monumental shift was something more...

Chapter 1

More Than Lee

M any people believe that the White Supremacist who came to our great city of Charlottesville were present because they did not agree with City Council's decision to remove the Robert E. Lee statue, but this wasn't the case. The decision for the Klu Klux Klan to come to the city on July 8th 2017 – and the arrival of the White Supremacists on August 11th and 12th – ran a course far deeper than what many could ever perceive.

Some know the truth, while others on the outside looking in can merely surmise. You see, Charlottesville isn't just a quaint and quiet college town that's ideal for weddings and famous for its collegial education. Racial inequality runs through its blood; our blood - under the shadow of Thomas Jefferson, Paul McIntire, and other 'polite' White Supremacists. Long before August 11th and 12th, covertly and overtly, White Supremacy has run rampant through our city and throughout Albemarle County. The controversy surrounding the statue was a manifestation of what was *always present*.

I, Wesley Jamont Bellamy, am living proof of that assertion, being only the seventh African American in our city elected to public office since the birth of Charlottesville in 1792. In fact, in Albemarle County, it's been nearly twenty years since the last person of color sat on the Board of Supervisors (Charles Martin was the last black person to serve on the Board in 2003). As it stands, due to these and other racial indiscretions throughout the city, it has been long believed amongst those who look like me, in Charlottesville, Albemarle, Orange, Fluvanna, Nelson, and the surrounding areas, representation in positions of power and influence are few and far in between.

People like myself are pushing to create change, however... change from a narrative begging to be rewritten that is not only loud but unafraid. Change intended to make some people uncomfortable, but that by which will also force those people to think critically, and to challenge the way things have been done before. Unfortunately, my efforts won't be the first of this town to advocate justice nor is it lost on me that those individuals almost always suffer vitriol and pushback.

When African Americans first tried to integrate the school system in Charlottesville in 1958, the citizens of the great city of Charlottesville resisted: an entire school division closed. The white folks within the city thought it better not to learn at all than to learn alongside Blacks (unless of course you had money, then you sent your children to the local private schools). Even more disturbing: When African Americans constructed a

2

thriving and prominent section within our community called Vinegar Hill – brick and mortar Black-owned businesses, schools, law offices, homes – in the name of "Urban Renewal", the city, or more notably the hate from within, tore it down. 139 homes owned by African Americans were destroyed. Nearly 30 Black-Owned businesses were destroyed. Not even a well-loved house of worship could stand against the anguish and fires of white supremacy.

Our stories, like that of so many other stories around the nation, and throughout history, of the efforts of African Americans being thwarted by oppressive means.

So, you may ask, what makes Charlottesville different then? From the histories of other Southern cities that share our stories of racial indifference and persecution? Little: just like any traditional town you may have read about in the books; Charlottesville and many surrounding areas have a history of racial disparities and is sadly reluctant to change. And like most places, there are educational gaps, serious poverty problems, and a lack of African Americans in governmental positions. Perhaps the only difference is, that before August 12th, a lot of people *believed* they were different.

That all said, I don't mean to suggest I haven't seen any positive change at all. Over the past couple of years, a new crop of leaders, both "homegrowns" and what some would call "transplants," have decided to step in, speak up, and speak out in bold, loud, and uncomfortable ways whenever the situation called for it. Elder leaders have been more open to sharing their past stories and encouraging the young to push for what's needed.

It's also been a long road, but we have seen White Supremacy be talked about, broken down into pieces, and slowly but surely dismantled through policy and activism. When one thinks about White Supremacy, we naively sometimes think of the Klu Klux *Klowns* being individuals hiding their faces with sheets, or idiots with tiki torches, but covert supremacy is often times entirely more vigilant. Which means that our efforts to thwart white supremacy must also evolve as well. For example, when we take a look at the amount of contract spending that is done with black businesses within the city, or the increasing number of minority businesses being founded within the city, it can be noted that we as a people have changed the policy to address previous issues.

Or when we look at our local schools and the number of black students who are in higher level classes, we have utilized activism of student leaders and adult activists to address the issue which leads the school board to make policy changes. When we see members of our community who choose to do things like wear confederate clothing in the wake of the White Supremacists attacks in Charlottesville, our school systems used policy to change this. And when we look at the need for more police accountability, a Civilian Review Board was created through policy to make this change.

Much of this work was done by African Americans in our

very community, by our people but it also has to be noted that we have had a lot of white allies who have used their privilege, their resources, and their time to assist with this push for change. So, as you can see though the road is long before us, we are – and I do mean all of us, are indeed walking it.

On December 15th, 2014, a few days after I led a protest from First Baptist Church on W. Main St. to the Downtown Mall with a list of "tangible" demands, a crowd looking to help African Americans marched on to the City Council meeting. Our normal procedure was for citizens to attend the meeting, sign up for three minutes, speak their peace, and then move on. Several people spoke. I then gave our list of demands and we all thought that we were on the right track, but a different group stood boldly and with vigor expressed concerns about police brutality and inequality, demanding, not asking, for change. Black, Brown, and White brothers and sisters took over the City Council meeting, and it was one of the first times that our Council saw anything like it. People would no longer accept business as usual.

After the meeting, I spoke with Dr. Holly Edwards, a local hero, and she said to me;

"Wes, it's not like we haven't been saying these things need to change for a long time. So, what, a curse word or two was used – have people never heard a curse word before? Do we have to yell and curse to get their attention? If so, then there is a *deeper* problem."

She was right, and I realized then that the energy was different. Feathers were ruffled, but that was only the beginning. In the subsequent months, pressure would continue to rise, but...

Black voices resounded.

In the shadows and in the valleys where people often didn't look, there was a group of people who were watching. Around our blue dot community, there was a sea of red who believed 'Black Lives Matter' was a terrorist organization and that Blacks were making too much noise. These shadows believed that they were losing power and influence as people of color rose up, that "their" city was changing... and not for the better.

Chapter 2

Wake Up

A fter being elected the 7th African American to our City Council, I noticed a few things were different. For starters, I was the youngest to be elected in our city's history, and though the first few months on the City Council went well enough, many saw me as an enthralled activist who would surely push for change. They weren't wrong, but that pressure alone was tremendous. To be honest, I was just a young man searching for his own identity and voice simultaneously trying to help the community find its own as well. On March 10, 2016 - less than three months into my first term on City Council as Vice-Mayor, I received a call that would ultimately change my life forever. In gist, the call went as such:

"Wes, we believe in you..." a young and kinetic voice emphasized. "...and now you have the opportunity to do something. Are you going to be about it? Or are you just going to talk about it like everyone else?"

"What happened?" I asked, not immediately understanding the passion behind the question.

"Did you see what Governor McAuliffe did today? You can do it. Now's the time."

I played it off as if I knew what Zhyana Bryant was talking about. What I didn't know was that Bryant, the 9th grade student activist who had a petition at her school to remove the statue of Robert E. Lee, who also saw me worthy enough to be the one person to whom which she thought to call to enact real change, would set the foundation for a battle long coming to Charlottesville. I then Googled it on my phone. My mouth dropped: Governor McAuliffe vetoed a bill that would have prevented the removal of Confederate Statues. And now the question that had been put to me, resonated:

...was I going to *be* about it or just *talk* about it?

I was instantly back in June 4th, 2013, at what was then known as "Lee Park." It was my first pursuit for a seat on City Council and I was doing one of the things that I liked to do the most: hosting a community cookout. It was a couple of days before the election, and I figured it would be a good time to drum up support and encourage everyone to head to the polls. The turnout was decent, but nowhere near the normal amount of people that usually attended these types of events. I didn't understand the decline until the next day at church. I was pulled to the side numerous times and reprimanded about how disrespectful it was for me to host a cookout in the same park where African-Americans were spat on, where a brother had his face slashed with a knife for walking through, where black kids were denied entry after leaving from the library – the stories didn't stop.

Receiving a tongue-lashing from the elders at several different churches a couple of days before your first election leaves a taste in your mouth that you can't just wash away with Sweet Tea and Lemonade. That Tuesday, there was a tie at the polls, and after a couple of recounts and it being discovered that there was a malfunction at one of the voting precincts, I lost the election by five votes. Eighty-seven people apologized to me for not voting because they were sure I was going to win, while twenty-one told me to my face that they didn't vote for me because it was obvious that I didn't understand the community: only a fool would tout himself as being our voice yet have a cookout in the place where we were never welcomed with a statue hoovering over it of a man who wanted to keep us enslaved.

With the history and countless stories of black oppression in Charlottesville in mind, it was no wonder why Bryant's words kept repeating in my mind:

"Are you going to be about it, or just talk about making change like everyone else before you?"

Charlottesville had been let down countless times before – whole communities left destitute and here I was in a position to either follow in those footsteps or make real change. I knew what I had to do, and prayer confirmed it. I called Kristin Szakos, my colleague on City Council, and asked her what she thought. She agreed the time was now: let's plan, execute, and challenge the status quo. Kristin was the change agent who, before I was on city council, was pushing forward with advocating for the city to not recognize Lee-Jackson Holiday. She received a ton of backlash for mentioning that in addition to no longer celebrating Lee-Jackson day, that one day the city should also think about removing the statue.

What I soon realized, however, that this was about more than a statue: it was about the people, those seldom heard. What lurked in the shadows, I didn't know, but I still geared up and readied for a fight to change the landscape of our city. It was the right thing to do.

Chapter 3

Decision Making

I knew this was a big decision, but I didn't know how big. It was March 2016, less than four months away from marrying my beautiful wife, Ashlee T. Bellamy and unbeknownst to me, my life was about to change. She had two daughters from a previous relationship and I already had a daughter: our Brady Bunch rendition was soon to become a reality. We had just purchased our first home together. I had, with ready anticipation, just moved from my Belmont bachelor pad and was more than ready to settle into my new life and home. We were up to our neck in boxes yet abundant in love... I was upstairs doing research at the time and talking to her on the phone.

"Looks like we'll have a chance to move the statue..." I told her, "and I think I'm going for it. Thoughts?"

"If that's what you want to do," she responded;
"Just be *careful*."

It was a warning... but I didn't think much about it at the time: honestly, you don't become an elected official at twenty-eight without some kind of ego. Throughout my

13

life, I had dealt with neighborhood shootouts, deaths, Federal agents taking away family members, and all kinds of adversity – I thought this was just another fight against White Supremacy, more of the same. Now that I look back on those memories, I realize now that everything was preparation for what was to come.

I'm often one of the people who is lauded, condemned, or labeled as the person who started the discussion about Confederate symbols in our city, but this isn't accurate. Several people had started the conversation long before me: Former City Councilors like Dr. Holly Edwards had discussed on several instances the need for us to come to grips with our past, and Council-woman Kristin Szakos, a mentor of mine for several years, also helped push the city to stop formally celebrating Lee-Jackson Day as of January 2015.

It was at that winter City Council meeting that I first tasted what vitriol that *"messing with"* the Confederate linage could cause – that meeting was beyond hectic. People, mostly white, drove in from all over Virginia to speak boldly about why they believed the holiday should remain instated and even before the meeting Kristin had received all kinds of hate mail. It quickly become clear that the statue was the last thing on the mob's mind: rather, they were more concerned about minorities, specifically black people, having a say on the agenda. Unfortunately, the City Council felt like they weren't out of their way to apologize for even bringing the issue up, and assured them that the stature was safe.

Funny how God works.

On March 10, 2016, I sent Kristin a text and said I needed to speak with her. We normally spoke two to three times a week, but rarely did I put an 'ASAP,' in the message. She understood the dire nature of the conversation and called right away. I asked her if she had seen what Gov. McAuliffe had done. She was initially caught off-guard as I was. We arranged to meet and spoke diligently about what McAuliffe's actions could mean for Charlottesville.

This was our chance.

Being the wise elder that she was, however, Kristin remained cautious – rightfully so. She wanted to speak through a variety of scenarios, speak with our legal department, do some more research, and most importantly, she wanted to look at it the entire situation more closely. She was a veteran on council and incredibly smart, and in many ways, I was probably her opposite. My youthful energy often came out in an inordinate amount of internal optimism, and I believed with every ounce of my body and spirit that this was the right thing to do. Kristin finally agreed, and we both decided that we would have to move fast.

We needed to involve community members, start a grass root effort, and be prepared for backlash. During the week, our City Manager, Maurice Jones, called me into his office and asked,

"Are you sure you understand what you're getting into?" he asked. And I replied the best I could;

"Yes."

Jones then showed me some of the hate mail that was sent to the city during the Lee-Jackson day situation. He warned me that things would be incredibly difficult for me, due to my skin color alone. And as much as I didn't want to believe it, I knew he wasn't wrong.

For a while, I had been fooling myself. I was the youngest person elected, the first to win all the precincts in the primary, and the leading vote-getter in both the Democratic primary and the General Election. My campaign slogan was "*Move the City Forward*", and I truly believed that the topic of race wasn't difficult because we lived in a liberal, progressive city that "just wasn't like that." The ghost of a lynched black man in the 1920s, the smell of gentrification and income disparity – I didn't think these existed in Charlottesville. The city was only nineteen-percent black and yet I had garnered the most votes, which meant numerous Whites voted me into office. That had to mean something, right? At the very least, it indicated that our great city was different... that we were at least *willing* to make the change, right?

But that day with Maurice Jones, the truth hit me all at once. The people who placed a monkey with bananas in front of my campaign signs, the people who voted for me but weren't ready to stop covert racism – they lived here.

The shadows were crowded.

It was all great when I was still known as the guy who teaches at the local high school, who held the boxing club for underprivileged youth, who was known mostly for speaking up within small community circles and providing an example of what happens when you "*work hard*." But then what happens when the black man, the one who wasn't from the commonwealth of Virginia challenges the status quo as an elected official? That is the caution that I saw in the eyes of Mr. Jones. It was almost like an older brother speaking to a younger brother. This was not a game. This was not for show. The journey that I was coming upon was bigger than just a statue. It was a battle for equity and challenging systems in ways that would make people think in ways that they were not prepared to. He asked me again, sternly and resolute: "...are you ready?"

My answer, repeated with vehemence, was the same.

"Yes."

Chapter 4

Beer and Water

The mission was clear now, and the objective was one that would be a tall task, but necessary. We were a city council that comprised of five members. Therefore, in order to get anything passed on the council three votes had to be earned. As Vice-Mayor of the city, the conversation needed to be had with our current mayor, Mike Signer. There were a lot of people who had different opinions on Mike, but I wanted to take a different approach as I had to work with him over the next four years. I was taking an approach that wanted to give the guy a chance. This was to the chagrin of a lot of people who I had looked up to. Mike, while serving as President of the Fifeville Neighborhood Association, one of the last black communities in the city, led an effort to try and get one of the liquor stores closed. You can do your own research to see how that played out, but I can say that it made a lot of people who I spoke to on a daily basis upset. There were a few hiccups with his campaign, but nonetheless he won a seat, and eventually became mayor of the city (the current city charter calls for the city council to appoint its own mayor and vice mayor, not by election from the public).

I believed that Mike was a pretty progressive guy, who for the most part, understood some of the deeper issues that plagued our city. I truly believed he would be on board with moving the statue, so I decided to call him and ask him if he wanted to chat. It was Friday, March 11th and I'll always remember thinking that this was all so surreal. We met at the downtown mall and had beer and water (everyone who knows me, knows that I don't drink... although, admittedly so, this job has almost made me do so on many a day).

So, there we were, the new city councilors, sitting at the mall sharing beverages that couldn't be anymore unalike much like our own personal policies – the irony. I decided now was the time and skipped the small talk and dived straight in. I told him about the idea to have the statue of Robert E. Lee removed, and how Governor McAuliffe had vetoed the bill which had essentially laid the path for us to be able to move the statue. Mike was initially caught off guard. He's a cerebral and an analytical guy so he wanted a variety of details about why, how, who, what, when, and where. We talked for maybe two hours, and I thought it was a good conversation. In fact, I walked away thinking that he was on our side. This was a defining moment in our relationship on council, but also in the movement of our city.

I can't stress enough that this wasn't at all about a statue, it was about true-blue equity. It was about people as a whole moving forward. It was also, most importantly about individuals doing what they believed to be right.

One thing that I distinctly remember taking away from that conversation was that not everyone moves at the same pace that I do. Some people like to listen, ask questions, be engaged, but still wait to make their own decision. And honestly, there was nothing wrong with that. But for the sake of Charlottesville –

I had to keep moving.

Chapter 5

A New Friend in The Movement

T hings were moving fast now. It was March 19th and we had heard that some guy named Bryan Stevenson was giving a talk at the Paramount Theater. In retrospect, I remember at the time I had no idea who he was. I remember the city buzzing about him coming to Charlottesville, and the tickets were damn near impossible to get. Luckily, I had a seat at the front, and I remember getting there late (I'm sure someone reading this will make a joke about me getting everywhere late, and that's ok too). About halfway through the talk, I felt something in my chest. This was divine timing. He was here, right now, providing a message to myself and the crowd of hopeful listeners – not by mistake. I am a firm believer that God does everything according to his will and purpose, and it was divine timing that Bryan Stevenson, civil rights leader, activist, thought provoker, and person who a lot of white liberal progressives trusted was here talking about how the ills of yesteryear affected us today. He wove in an out of breaking down historical misnomers while giving personal anecdotal testimony about life in the south. He was brilliant. My heart was full while listening to him, and while he was talking, I took a moment to look around at the crowd –

23

nearly 750 seats all full of people who were here to listen and learn about how race and history still played a role in our society. They were, as I was, hanging on to every bit of hope being pushed through his words. It will forever be a defining moment in my life and a time that I will absolutely never forget.

I thought to myself right then... I *have* to ask him an important question. See, Mr. Stevenson discussed the confederacy and the treacherous ways of the old south in his talk. He said something that resonated heavily with me: *"To create change, we have to become comfortable with being uncomfortable. Change is hard, but it's necessary."* I figured if we wanted to get more momentum about what we were trying to do in regards to moving the statue and creating more equitable spaces in our city, that Brian could be the man to do it.

If he approached the topic during one of his talks in front of all of those people, it would set the stage that we needed it to. However, I also thought to myself that it could be tremendously dangerous if it backfired. If he instead, said that he thought that the statues should stay, his opinion alone would be what a lot people (both white and black) who did not want to "stir up trouble" would use as a reason for cause to keep things as they were. I figured however, that it was still worth a shot, and that everything we'd worked towards up until that moment could rest right here in he

Mr. Stevenson finished his speech and the moderator let us know that we only had time for a couple of questions. I figured it was now or never, and raised my hand. I don't know if it was because I was in the front, or because I was an elected official, or if it was just a small bit of fate, but the microphone was brought over to me.

All eyes were on me.

I introduced myself and got a little cheer, which helped calm my nerves, and I proceeded to ask him;

"You mentioned a great deal about images and symbols from the past having lingering effects on localities. We have a huge statue of Robert E. Lee in a city park right up the street. Do you think it should stay there? Regardless of your answer, I want to invite this entire theatre to Lee Park on Tuesday at 9:00 AM as myself and Councilor Kristin Szakos host a press conference to announce that we are moving forward with a plan to remove that statue."

Mr. Stevenson paused for a moment, quite possibly thinking carefully about what he should say – which wrecked my nerve for half a second as I waited in anticipation, but then he finally responded calmly, "Yes, you're right. I agree. They should be removed."

The crowd cheered for a moment. Which was a HUGE sigh of relief on my part. He later went on to talk about how there was no need for these statues, that were

25

mostly put up to show direct defiance of African-American upward mobility and were problematic from conception. We had the opportunity to chat after the event was over, and he encouraged Kristin and I to keep pushing and to let him know if we needed anything, but he had done enough. He allowed the tone to be set.

I remember getting phone calls and texts that night from people saying that they never really thought about the statue being moved, but because of what I asked and what Stevenson agreed to, now considered it the right thing to do. That was the general consensus amongst a lot of people that I encountered. Many would say over the next few days, *"Wes, I never really thought about it like that. I mean do we really have those issues here in Charlottesville?"* or *"That statue has been up for almost 100 years, how is it a problem?"*

It was clear, we were still operating in the sunken place. At that point and time, we refused to even acknowledge that there was an issue of any sort, let alone be willing to deal with the issue. That wasn't my problem though. It wasn't my job to wake everyone up at once, it was my job to get the car on the highway to drive towards equity and consciousness. That's a long highway, mind you, and I was learning, that my seat belt needed to be fastened. I remember thinking that we were halfway there, and this wasn't going to be that long of a ride. While some people were lost, the majority of people understood the issue at hand, and understood why this was important.

The car ride was still in the infant stages. The journey was literally just beginning, and... it was about to get real.

Dr. Wes Bellamy

Chapter 6

No Turning Back Now:

Formal Announcement at the City Council Meeting

Sunday, March 20th - The proverbial cat was out of the bag and the city was buzzing about the idea of the statue being moved. I had already spoken with most of the African-American Pastors in the city, and asked for them to give me five minutes of the service to encourage people to come to the city council meeting and/the press conference on Tuesday morning. I sent out an email blast to everyone that I knew in the city, and I had put it up on my social media. There was no turning back at this point.

This also meant that there was a large contingent of people who did not like what I was doing. I will never forget walking up the steps to one of the churches and seeing a couple of men that I *really* looked up to. A contingent of older African-American gentleman who I had known for several years stopped me and gave me the usual talk, they're proud of me, praying for me, and were insisting that I keep a level head. One in particular asked what was I doing over at the service since there was nothing special going on. I told him about the idea of moving the statue and that I wanted to come over to

29

encourage the congregation to come out and support. His words sliced me deeper than a chef at Ruth Chris...

"Them people ain't going to let you do that, Wes. I've been here my entire life. I know they ain't. Just forget it. Ain't nothing around here going to change anytime soon. Them people going to think what they think, and do what they do. You've been doing well. Just keep working with the kids. Keep being on city council. Don't stir anything up. This is only going to cause trouble. Trust me, I've been here my whole life. Ain't nothing going to change."

I wasn't prepared to hear that. I literally stopped in my tracks and the only thing that I could do to respond was put on a fake smile and say, "Well, it's my job to try. Things have to change. I have to try."

I knew that I had to keep my composure because I was walking into one of the most historic churches in the area and the people would expect me to be my usual happy and optimistic self. But on the inside, I wanted to cry. The psyche of our people had been damaged so much that most of us felt it was better to simply lay down and be quite opposed to stand up and fight for what's right. These were the kind of things that I had read about in different books, or articles, or heard stories about, but in my naivety, I didn't think that it would happen to me. That people whom I looked up too would look down upon me in such a way. I'm not sure why I didn't believe that Black people in Charlottesville wouldn't be afraid to challenge the system similar to other traditionally southern cities, but I did. I thought that they would instantly follow me. I thought that they would be prepared to fight for what's right immediately. I believed that we would stand up no matter what. I was wrong.

I stood at the church doors contemplating his words and thinking about this long trip ahead, this journey, this pilgrimage of sort which was still very much in the early phases. I wondered was I really prepared for what was to come. It wasn't about the statue - it was about changing the culture of the city. My city. And empowering those who felt powerless, pissing off those who had always maintained the power, and getting the ones in the middle to understand that being on the right side of justice required more than just a few nice words here or there. It was going to courage... and a lot of it.

I finally walked into the church that morning, carrying his words and my thoughts in my chest and using them as a battery of sorts to fuel my passion. My speech, my words, came plummeting out through my mouth like a raging bull in desperate need of a target:

"I *need* you. I need you all to come to the city council meeting tomorrow. I need you to come to the press conference on Tuesday. I need you to be there with us. I need you to be there with me. This isn't about me, it's about changing the culture of this city. It's about us being able to be free and welcome in any and every part of our city. We don't have to accept this, we can stand up! And we *can* fight it!"

Some cheered and clapped, some yawned, some just stared at me like I was crazy. The passion I had just felt tumbled off of me and ran away like a defeated child. That was all in just the first two church visits. By the time I had got to church number three, my home church, First Baptist on W. Main St., I was psychologically all over the place. However, I walked in there was a new sense of motivation. The energy was different. Probably because my Pastor, Hodari Hamilton, who had been my confidant throughout it all, was giving a sermon about how it was our duty from God to stand up and fight for what's right. Hodari was more than my pastor, he was more like my brother. This was my home church. Pastor Hamilton and his family were lifelines of sorts for my family. Actually, thinking back on it, it's like something out of a movie or story book. The pastor and the politician. We talked about everything. He was a social justice and fire spitting pastor if there ever was one. Never afraid to speak up. Never afraid to encourage others that God called us to stand tall. Pastor and I are, to a certain extent, the same person, just in different lanes. Our birthdays are on the same date. Our passion for change the same. Our ideas often big but intentions pure. Even our pursuit to be bold change agents were always aligned.

So, when I walked into our church, shortly after the sermon had started and took my seat at in the front row, Pastor Hamilton must have picked up on my energy. I firmly believe that God makes no mistakes, and he gave Hodari the words to pick up my spirit. After his sermon, I felt a burst of energy come over me. This was the right thing to do. We had to push to make people uncomfortable. Sitting idle and just praying for change wasn't going to do anything. Faith without works is dead. We had to put action behind our prayer for equity in our city. This could no longer wait. We had to act. At the end of Pastor Hamilton's sermon, he did the alter call, and final prayer. He then asked everyone to stay for a few moments after church because Brother Wes needed to speak to everyone. He spoke briefly about how important it was for the church to support me on city council and city endeavors. This put me at ease.

In my mind, it was divine.

This was also one of the pivotal moments in the entire saga. Our Mayor, Mike Signer, was also at service to talk about a matter pertaining to W. Main St. Pastor Hamilton finished up his sermon and called me up. I made the same passionate speech that I had at all of the other churches, but this time I let my church family know that there was something tangible that they could do right here and right now:

"If you want the statue to be moved, if you want equity in all city parks, if you want to stand up for what's right, let your mayor know. *He's sitting right there.*"

Mike was pissed to say the least. People began to say different things to him, and in my mind, it was an empowering moment for the community. Rarely did they interact with the mayor, and now they were able to get some of the issues that we had been dealing with for generations off of their chest in a controlled setting. I thought it was great... Mike, not so much. He eventually made his way up to the podium to discuss W. Main St., but by the time he did, most of the congregation had left. In my own eagerness to get people to be involved in the process – to engage them, to motivate them, to energize them around what I wanted to do... I stole the show and sucked all of the air out of the room. I thought it was good strategy, but he saw it as me throwing a grenade at the situation to pressure him into doing what I wanted him to, and he was adamant that nobody, myself included, would force him to do anything. I think it was at that moment that he began to sink his heels in the dirt, and the fight was on. It's getting real. Not only am I fighting the confederates, the moderates who thought the statue was art, the people who thought that we never had any racial issues in Charlottesville, but I'm also fighting my colleague on city council, our mayor.

Monday, March 21 - To be honest, I don't remember much about the city council meeting that night. The entire day had been a blur. The word was all the way out that the press conference was Tuesday, and the lovers of the Confederacy were blowing up my social media, my city council cell phone, and it seemed like everyone had something to say about it. The energy in the area was different. I wasn't really worried or concerned yet. I'm not sure why. I had spoken with Governor McAuliffe, had spoken with the State Police, had spoken with local police, and was also getting a lot of messages from friends around the way that they were going to be there, and they were going to make sure that I was safe by any means necessary. I was just thinking that everyone is making a big deal out of it. It's probably going to be around 50 or so people in total, we will say our peace, and then we will leave. At the end of the city council meeting, Kristin and I formally announced that we would be hosting a press conference to formally pursue all options to remove the statue of Robert E. Lee from Lee park, and place it in a more appropriate setting. However inside of the council chambers, something was different. When I left the meeting, I remember thinking in my mind that maybe this was the start of something. I wasn't sure what, but it was the start of something.

I was hoping that it was the beginning of change.

Chapter 7

And So, It Begins

Actual language from Press Conference:

Unity in the Community: Removal of General Lee

Statue and Renaming of Lee Park

Charlottesville -- On Tuesday, March 22nd at 9:30
AM, community leaders from across the city of
Charlottesville will come together to urge Charlottesville
City Council to pursue the action of renaming Lee Park
and removing the statue of General Robert E. Lee.

Community leaders are calling for the
removal of the statue and renaming of the
park based on the grounds that:

37

1) General Lee has no historical ties to the city of Charlottesville.

2) The statue was donated by Paul McIntire on May 21, 1924 during a time period in which it was plausible to believe that the values and core beliefs of those in positions of leadership differed from the current leadership. Several current residents have stated that they believe the statue was used as a psychological tool to show dominance of the majority over the minority during this time period. Subsequently, a large portion of city residents have refused to step foot in Lee Park due to what they believe the statue and park represent. A disrespect to one group of people is a disrespect to all, and the city of Charlottesville has a responsibility to help all who dwell in the city feel welcomed, respected, and included.

3) As Governor McAuliffe has vetoed House Bill 587, Governor Terry McAuliffe has vetoed legislation that would prevent Virginia localities from taking down monuments to the Confederacy and other war-related memorials, saying it would prohibit communities from making their own decisions about controversial symbols.

In a veto announced Thursday, March 10th, McAuliffe said he supports historic preservation, but called the legislation a "sweeping override of local authority" that has ramifications for "interpretive signage to tell the story of some of our darkest moments during the Civil War."

"There is a legitimate discussion going on in localities across the commonwealth regarding whether to retain, remove, or alter certain symbols of the Confederacy," McAuliffe said in his veto message. "These discussions are often difficult and complicated. They are unique to each community's specific history and the specific monument or memorial being discussed. This bill effectively ends these important conversations."

This action has been discussed on several occasions, and with the recent development in Richmond, the city of Charlottesville has an opportunity to act. The goal of this press conference is to show a united front to the constituents of Charlottesville, while also asking for city leaders to make a concerted effort to create an inclusive and welcoming environment for all throughout the city.

In addition to the press conference, a petition has been started by Charlottesville High School student Zyahna Bryant which can be found here:

https://www.change.org/p/charlottesville-city-council-change-the-name-of-lee-park-and-remove-the-statue-in-charlottesville-va

Chapter 8

The Day I Went to Hell and Back

That Tuesday began just like most other Tuesday's. I woke up around 5:30 am to go and play basketball with my friends. We lifted weights afterwards. I showered, changed and then I headed over to the park. I was scheduled to speak at 9:30 am and everything was already set up. The mics were good, the sound was secured, the speakers were set, so basically, all I had to do was show up. I said a prayer before leaving the gym, turned on Jeezy's "Trap or Die" intro and made my way. As I was driving up, scoping out the 150 individuals in attendance, I realized suddenly, that *THIS* was what everyone was talking about and there it stood, hoovering over the crowd...

The Robert E. Lee statue.

There was a large group of people with Confederate flags, waving them all over the park as they shouted. After I parked my car, the state troopers immediately surrounded me and said that they would be escorting me everywhere that I go for the duration of the day. One of my brothers from the 100 Black Men, Pastor Rickey White, also walked with me. We said a prayer, and it all hit me. The people who came to the press conference

41

were not there to defend the statue. They were there because they felt that there was an attack on their culture and their way of life.

As myself, Rickey and the troopers to whom were escorting furthered our way into the park, a man walked up to me and introduced himself as Wesley. This Wesley, was the commander of the regional Sons of the Confederacy, and he wanted to have a moment with me.

I'm fresh out of the gym, fresh off of a prayer, and in my mind, ready for whatever. Wesley asked if we could speak in private, and I obliged. He said to me;

"I just want you to know that I may not agree with you on this removing the statue, but I can see how it would make you and people who are like you offended. My family fought in the Civil War. I love my heritage, but I don't hate anyone. Some people here just hate you. I'm not one of them. I have a lot of respect for you."

I was absolutely floored by his comments. It was the kind of thing that let me know that God was present. We took a couple of pictures together shaking hands before departing from one another. He went his way, back to the crowd, and I went mine, continuing my way down the long stretch to the podium. That interaction made me think of what the statue of Robert E. Lee symbolized and who the people with all of the confederate flags actually were. For some, the statue was symbolic as it meant that the South would rise again. It meant that this was *their* home. I've been told repeatedly that there were only a handful of men who walked the earth that were better men than Robert E. Lee, and one of them was said to be able to walk on water. So, saying that we were going to move this statue and change the name of the park was unfathomable. They had heard rumblings about people saying they would do this or that in years past, but now there were actually two elected officials who had a plan that they planned to execute. This also was about race.

Make no mistake about it, the fact that I was Black, that I was boisterous, and that I wasn't backing down – in the eyes was extremely problematic.

I took another moment to look upon the crowd and saw, not only the sea of Confederate flags but also people holding signs with everything you can imagine on one side of the park. On the other side, there were about 20 young women from a local school, and another mixed crowd of 80-100 people from the community who wanted to see the statue go. The crowd was definitely mixed. African Americans, Latinx, young, old, clergy, homeless, and everyone else in between were in attendance. I scanned the crowd again and felt a sudden sense of urgency come over me. I checked in with Szakos who had already spoken with the list of speakers who we had lined up for the event. Everything was going according to plan, it was in that moment that I realized the urgency I was feeling was less about the organization of the event but rather my ancestors – our ancestors, channeling through me a sense of power and readiness. I felt them without question that day. And I embraced their presence... because I was going to need it.

The first speaker came, Zyahna Bryant, the passionate and brilliant young leader who initially started the petition to remove the statue as well as continued to speak to me about the need to create change. She spoke with such conviction and truth that I was more than inspired. She looked into the eyes of those who hated her and stood tall. She finished her speech and was unafraid. She was, and remains an American hero. The next speaker came, and things appeared to be rather calm. Some were upset, but there wasn't any direct confrontation up until that point. I was actually pleased with how things were going. Things took an immediate turn for the worse however, after my sister, Amy Sarah Marshall spoke.

Amy, who is the chair of the Charlottesville PRIDE organization, spoke about her experiences as a young woman growing up in the deep south, not being able to fully express herself and take pride in her identity and how the statue of Robert E. Lee did not represent her, her values or our city. She was immediately met with resistance from the people who held the large confederate flags. She was called all kinds of names, as they berated and yelled at her. The entire mood of the press conference had shifted. It was now clear that this was not going to be the kind of event that was going to go smoothly. Amy was understandably startled and I

44

stepped in after she finished to remind the crowd that this was not the kind of event in which we would tolerate such behavior.

People appeared to listen and calmed down enough for Amy to finish her speech and leave the podium. The next speaker, Dr. M. Rick Turner, however, would not be intimidated easily. Turner was the President of the Charlottesville-Albemarle NAACP. Standing at 6'3, with a deep baritone that he often spoke with boisterously and loud, his presence and demeanor alone commanded respect. After watching the initial response to Amy Sarah, he stepped to the podium and reiterated that the NAACP was the oldest civil rights organization in the country, and that they stand up for all people in need when they were being bullied. Obviously perturbed by the treatment of the last speaker, Dr. Turner proceeded to speak on how the heritage of African-Americans in Charlottesville has often been disrespected, rarely acknowledged, and in more cases than not, how black people in our community were treated as second class citizens. He described the statue of Robert E. Lee as one of the most disrespectful items that could be in a public party, and the statue deserved to be in a trash can.

You can imagine, in regards to civility, all bets were off. As Turner stepped down from the podium unphased by the savagery of the crowd, not even Pastor Hodari Hamilton could calm them down. Try as he might, he spoke about the need for love and mentioned how justice and truth went hand and hand. People attempted

45

to shout over him, and by the time my fellow colleague, Kristin, came up to speak, those who opposed the statue being moved, were more than livid. She held her composure though and said her peace, and then she passed me the microphone. For some reason, in that moment, the detractors initially stopped yelling as if they wanted to hear what I had to say.

I began my speech by speaking about the need for people to be brave enough to pursue change –

"...It's not easy, but I cannot stand idle and look both young people and our elders in the eye and not do anything to address the deep pain that they had expressed to me about this park and statue..." I added.

This infuriated many of those who stood with the Confederate flags. They began to call me coward, communist, some were literally yelling about how they felt disrespected and I was not being fair because I was not allowing them the opportunity to talk. I reminded them that this was not their press conference throughout my speech, and did my best to focus on the message. But this was not about a statue... This was about a group of people who felt that their way of life was being challenged. Here I was, a 28-year-old "transplant" who had only been in Virginia for 5 years, a black man telling them that their statue needed to be removed and the name of the park needed to be changed. Never did I mention that we were going to destroy the statue. Never did I say that we were going to desecrate the statue. In actuality, **I said that the statue would be better suited in a museum or public park so that it could be admired in the proper context by whomever wanted to admonish it.** However, I realized again, that this wasn't about Robert E. Lee at all.

The look in the faces of the people who were there were reminiscent of the things that my grandmother and relatives in South Carolina and Georgia told me about in the early to mid-1900s. The looks on their faces were those reminiscent of what we saw in history books and documentaries. I was also reminded that Charlottesville was not the place where things like this happened, and the topic of race was not one that was to be talked about. It was to be whispered about. Challenging the status quo or even demanding that black people be treated as equals was seen as an immediate threat. Yes, our community may vote Blue and we believed that we were progressive, but our values were deeply rooted in traditional southern beliefs. Beliefs that meant that people of color, specifically black people were seen as inferior. I knew that I couldn't stand idle.

The people in the comment sections of the local news outlets who asked about the change in our city, along with the people who sent in hate mail and negativity were all here now in my face, all looking for answers on either side and I knew that I couldn't back down. I looked around at the sea of Confederate Flags and people with signs with my name on it and I stood my ground. Finished my speech and stood steadfast in my beliefs not because of opportunity but because I had no other choice but to do what was right for those here watching and for the generations to come. The moment was now – right now.

I thought about the story of the elder who told me about her brother who was close to my age in the 1960s and having his face slashed for walking in the same park that I stood up in declaring that a statue would be removed. When the elders said to me that they were afraid for me, this is what they spoke of. When we speak up and speak out, we come under attack. Those attacks or methods of intimidation can be physical, mental, online, or even in detrimental ways like going after our very livelihood. Deciding to speak up and challenge those who have traditionally been in positions of power has not traditionally went well for us. As the people decades before me would say, "This could stir up a lot of trouble." But while speaking that day, I looked to my left, and behind me. I saw a sea of students who didn't look like me, but stood there with me. I saw a crowd of people of different races, ethnicities, and a variety of labels that made us "different" stand together and also chant/cheer for us to do what is right. The tide was changing. They reminded me of the abolitionist, the freedom riders, the people who would rather walk out of school and protest in the street than be treated as a second-class citizen.

This was the beginning of the "New Charlottesville." The place where we put equity first. The place where we decided to collectively use our voices. It may look like most of this was about a statue, but it's not. It's about a

48

community and area as a whole that is changing. It's about boldly challenging the dark ghosts of the past and the covert and overt oppression of the present. The change that we were striving for would not be easy. As we saw, just to even talk about the change that we were pursuing would be met with staunch opposition, but it was necessary. For my children, for your children, for our grandchildren, this was a must. This was day one for me. This was the long road to change in our city.

So, as I think about August 12th. I think about the events like on this date, and the days thereafter. I think about the direction that our community has gone in the months thereafter. I think about the change that has occurred. I think about the progression. I think about the work ahead. One phrase comes to mind;

"Be patient with people, but impatient with progress."

Dr. Wes Bellamy

Chapter 9

The Day After

O nce the press conference was over, I was rushed out by the state police and Pastor Rickey White. Thankfully so, needless to say the crowd was in arms after I left the podium. I was also scheduled to go to Hampton, Virginia right away for a recruitment event for Albemarle County Public Schools in an attempt to try and persuade more African-American teachers to come to the school division. Emotionally, I was all over the place. I felt liberated and proud, but I was also still in shock. Processing what had just happened during a two-hour drive, it was clearer than ever. This was not going to be a quick and easy policy change. My phone began to ring off the hook. A lot of people were calling to ask if I was ok, but I wasn't. I pretended that I had it all figured it out. I pretended that I had a sense of confidence that almost guaranteed that I wasn't rattled, but I was. I looked on social media, and my chest got tight. The images and videos of the event as a whole played out like a horror movie. The scenes – parts of the park in conflict, people angry and yelling amongst each other, and the fighting – hundreds of clips of pieces of violence that I hadn't seen by being up at the podium. It was more chaotic than I

51

ever imagined. I placed my phone face down on the car seat just to get a peace of mind. After finally arriving in Hampton, I tried to take my mind off of things in Charlottesville, and do what I originally set out to – bring more teachers of color to our school division. Normally while in the "757" - like people affectionately call the area, I link up with friends and family. We go out to eat or laugh and joke, or do something to fulfill our time. This trip was different. I stayed in my hotel room the entire visit until it was time to go home the next morning. Flipping through the channels, I stumbled upon the local news and there I was on the top headline story. More and more, it's registering that this was a really big deal.

Some people have said to me or about me, that I originally wanted to push for this because I wanted to make a name for myself or because I wanted some attention. I can honestly say that's not true. Now in truthfulness, I did hope that some people in the local area would take note of the efforts and feel empowered to speak up about the things that they saw that were wrong where they lived. I prayed that this would let people know that we, Black people, didn't have to simply take what was given to us. We can take on a variety of battles, let our voice be heard, and win. What that translated to and how it actually would play out, I wasn't quite sure. I was just hoping that people in the area would continue to stand tall.

Now, here I was... sitting in a hotel suite two hours away from home and watching myself on the television screen.

It felt good, but it also meant that there would be a bigger bullseye on my chest and back. My Instagram, Twitter, and Facebook were inundated with trolls and idiots who were calling me all kinds of things – "Nigger" of course, being at the top of the list. I was being told that I should be hung for questioning the great Robert E. Lee. This was startling, but to be expected. I can say now looking back at it, it was necessary. See up until this point, I really didn't get a lot of pushback. Of course, I had the usual detractors say negative things every now and again, but in my opinion, that was of the norm. Now, the voices and criticism came from a variety of different angles – hate-filled corners with evil on their minds and tongues. It was loud but I realized that my skin had to be tougher.

The next few days were a complete whirlwind. Charlottesville was in a new space. My students asked me upon returning back to the city; *"Mr. B., why do you want to take down the statue? My mom said this about it, my dad said this about it, they said they don't like you…"* while others were extremely supportive. Some students even sent me letters with words of encouragement which warmed my heart. And some community members made a concerted effort to ensure that I knew that I had their support. The feeling in the air of the city made it feel as if we were definitely bubbling upon something and going down unchartered waters. We were now dealing with the topic of race in a way that we never have before. The conversation was not only open but was happening everywhere – In the grocery stores, in the barbershops, in the schools, on the playgrounds, in the restaurants, in the shared spaces, and in our private enclaves... Even more reassuring, it also appeared that everyone had an opinion which meant that this discord was not just falling on deaf ears. As a whole, very few people knew the actual history behind the statue of Robert E. Lee in Lee Park. There were several layers that had to be peeled back first, but being able to at the very least discuss what was happening on the surface meant that people were open to change. And that was a great sign.

In the following days I began to be questioned for my initial involvement in wanting to move the statue in the first place, outside of the obvious pull from community outreach. In the original press release and in all of my initial statements I attempted to lay out the reasoning for why the statue didn't belong. Robert E. Lee never fought in Charlottesville, we don't have any direct historic ties to the civil war, not to mention the statue was put up by a man, Paul McIntire who vehemently believed that African Americans were inferior, and the fact that the KKK and other proud racists lauded the statue during the time of its unveiling. This wasn't enough though.

Not only was the statue a constant topic of discussion, they wanted more from me. My community wanted more, my political opposition wanted more and even the

54

naysayers wanted more but no one was willing to do the work *with* me to see this majestic change everyone was now buzzing about. During this time period, a lot of people don't like to read or do the research to understand the deeper issues that plagued our area. A lot of people weren't prepared to think critically about the situation as a whole. And that bothered me.

So, I decided to run a campaign on moving the city forward by being a conduit or bridge of sorts between groups and pockets of people that rarely interacted. I thought perhaps by placing contrasting social groups together, it would help people understand our differences are only skin deep and to *do the work*.

I traditionally played in the BCBA Men's basketball league at Tonsler Park, a traditional African-American Park that conjured hundreds of people from different communities together on Sunday afternoons to hang out, talk trash, watch brothers play ball, and have a moment to embrace the African-American culture that we all knew and loved in Charlottesville. I also found myself attending more and more house parties in places like Park St., a traditionally wealthy community of affluent Whites in the city. At that time, I was supposed to be the young guy who was going to help both sides understand each other. I was supposed to play it safe. I was supposed to focus on what brings us together and never bring up what makes us different. I was supposed to be focus solely on the great parts of Charlottesville while in some circles, but still work my ass off to address inequities in other pockets. I felt that a lot of people of affluence thought that I was some kind of super negro that they thought was a unicorn that they could send a few dollars to a cause and that freed them from dealing with the real issues in our city. I can't tell you how many times I heard;

"Wes, you're doing such a great job with those at-risk youth." I hate the term At-risk, by the way. Or "Wes, your community is really lucky to have you. You're so articulate, and smart, and a real example."

And on the surface, some would hear that and think that they should feel special. I definitely drank that sweet tea, and believed that I was the chosen one. But the more that I thought about the fact that our city had a 27% poverty rate for several years. The more I looked at the kids that I mentored and broke down the educational disparities, the health disparities, and the differences in quality of life for young people who lived within a 10.5 square mile city, the more I realized that the covert ways of systemic racism at play. The more that I interacted with people from around the different neighborhoods of poverty and realized that they were living in a cycle that perpetuated dependency on systems and entities and rarely promoted equitable solutions for upward mobility, the more upset I became.

As I sat back and analyzed the things that people would say to me in regards to being a conduit, the more I felt that they believed this was my job, and not ALL of our responsibility. They were comfortable with having the new, young, energetic, articulate, black male who came with solutions, because it meant that they didn't have to address their own internal bias. A lot of people in my position believe that as long as we are the ones that people come to for solutions, that our positions are solidified, and we can remain relevant. That's a fallacy, because it shows that we are only a pawn in the continued oppression of our people.

So, why did decide to risk it all on a statue they ask? And when am I going to do more? Well, what's the topic that would force as many people as possible to look at the real systemic issues within our community and in an honest way look at the topic of race and would lead to all of us doing *more*... the statue.

The city, county, region, and state were now talking about race in ways that they didn't even understand that they were doing. That's the first step. Start the conversation, which in some instances is the hardest part because some will use every excuse imaginable to dodge the topic. That goes for both Black and White people. The topic is so polarizing that it essentially becomes taboo. Everyone knows what's going on, but few want to talk about it. Now we were in a position that we forced them to. Yes, it was tough, but overall, necessary.

Chapter 10

The Making of An Enemy:

Black Supremacist in the Eyes of Some

n the days, weeks, and months after the initial press conference, things were definitely different. The mood in the city was different. The energy was something unlike anything that I had seen before. Some people were feeling empowered – loudly questioning the need for the statue of Robert E. Lee in the middle of our city. Some were doing research and understanding how the KKK loudly and proudly marched through our city during the days shortly before and after the statue was erected. The stories about inequity were being told and we were now in a position to figure out how to deal with it. By that same token, there were still a lot of people who didn't like what was happening. There was a large contingent of people of different races, ages, and ethnicities who believed that "history can't be changed" therefore maintaining that the statue shouldn't be removed.

As it would seem, If I wasn't before, I was now one of the most polarizing figures in the area. There really wasn't much of an in-between, either people loved me, or they hated me. I was moving around in the city and the area, trying to keep a level head and pretend that things were ok, but they weren't. I vividly remember the death threats, the letters in the mail, the phone calls, the messages, and I knew that this was more serious than I ever imagined. However, I was at the point in which there was no turning back. I prayed daily, and eventually, I became at peace with it all. I realized that this was God's will for my life. This is what I was made to do. Don't hide, don't run, don't cower, embrace it. So that's what I did. Once I adopted that mindset, things began to change. I was appointed to the Virginia State Board of Education, I was named one of 12 New Deal Progressive Leaders (A national honor), my wife and I got married in July of 2016 in a lovely celebration with friends and adorning family. Things were moving very fast, there was a lot more attention, and even more responsibility, but I was happy. I was comfortable with who I was becoming. A civil rights leader was never a title that I sought after, but as it become more and more apparent that this was the light that most people saw me in, I wanted to accept it.

A lot of people think that the Unite the Right Rally began about the statue, but I vehemently disagree. As aforementioned, the topic of race had been one that had been brewing and bubbling for several years, but now it was in the forefront. We couldn't hide from it anymore. The leader of the Unite the Right Rally, was a man named Jason Kessler. Kessler has/had made it his life mission to destroy me. In a sense it's as if he's obsessed with me. In all honesty, I never even knew who the guy was until October of 2016. Some will disagree, but in my opinion, it was during this time that the mood of our community took a shift for the worse. This was the time period where Jason Kessler found his voice.

The old adage, that God works in mysterious ways is one of the truest statements of all times. Alicia Garza, Co-Founder of the Black Lives Matter Movement, came to Charlottesville in early October 2016. I remember really wanting to go to her talk at the Paramount Theater, but missing my opportunity to do so because I promised some of my mentees that we would play basketball that same evening. I had never met her, had heard a lot about her, and admittedly, wanted to see what all of the hype was about. Little did I know that Alicia would later become one of my closest confidants and encouragers, but at this point and time, she was a woman who came to the city to speak on the social and racial unrest, and discuss the movement for Black Lives.

Shortly after her talk, my phone was blowing up from people throughout the city and area. I finished hooping and saw about 20 missed calls and several social media notifications and got a little worried that I had did something wrong. But it wasn't me, it was actually a person who I had come to know and respect named Doug Muir who had put his proverbial foot in his mouth on Facebook. Doug Muir, was amongst many things; a venture capitalist in the area, a professor at the

University of Virginia, and owner of the restaurant known as Bellas. For some reason - some God awful reason, Doug decided to comment on a Facebook post about Alicia's speech. He wrote:

"Black lives matter is the biggest rasist [sic] organisation [sic] since the clan [sic]. Are you kidding me. Disgusting!!!'"

My phone was going crazy because earlier in the year Doug and I served on a panel together, got a chance to know each other, and I had publicly said on several occasions that he was a good guy. My initial thoughts were that he was hacked. I remember thinking, there was no way he had said those things. "Absolutely no way. The spelling doesn't even look right. Can't be him." I thought to myself. People and groups, including the local NAACP and Black Lives Matter contingent, were asking of me my thoughts and I wanted to take a moment or two to do some fact finding. I reached out to a few mutual friends to try and speak with Doug, and eventually after a few days, I managed to track him down to have two conversations with him. He in fact made the statements, and I told him that while I appreciated him speaking with me, and agreeing to go through some sensitivity training, at this point, it was a little late.

The local NAACP had planned a protest outside of his restaurant, and was calling for the community to come out and join them. I also put out a statement on Instagram (because that's where millennials put out their

62

press releases) condemning Doug's words, supporting the boycott, and reminding people that we had to use our collective buying power to send messages that certain things were not going to be tolerated. I initially thought that I was simply adding my two cents, but I didn't quite take into account the power of influence of my voice at the time as it pertained to my position. It's one thing for Wes Bellamy, the activist and member of the community to call for a boycott, it's another for Wes Bellamy, the Vice-Mayor of a city to call for one.

Looking back at it all, I think this is part of what enraged a different demographic of detractors. Those who said enough was enough. There were a group of people who already didn't like me because of the statue, and were looking for new reasons to bring me down a peg or two. Admittedly, I can't deny that my head was bigger than a man on the moon, and it often showed. This only added fuel to the fire. The push against me was that an elected official should not lead a boycott or protest against a city business. I thought it was a ridiculous claim for several reasons. Right is right, and wrong is wrong. To compare Black Lives Matter, a group that was founded to inform the community that our lives have value, to stand up to the oppressive systems that were created to hold us back, and to be a voice for the oppressed to the Klu Klux Klan was one of the most disrespectful things that anyone could ever say. Those words, said by a man as accomplished as Doug Muir in present time, needed to be addressed and had to have consequences.

Furthermore, before I was ever an elected official, I was, and still am, a black man who has to navigate in a society that sees my value and other brothers like me, as less than, every step of the way. For those reasons, because I had/have the platform, I felt obligated in my soul to use it to speak up and speak out against oppressive microaggressions.

I was originally planning to not attend the protest, as I had a speech already planned in Louisa County for their NAACP Freedom Fund banquet. However, after picking up my daughters from camp at our church, which was literally across the street from Bellas, I decided to walk over. I wanted them to see what a protest looked like. I wanted them to understand what Dad was often fighting for, and to also know that I wasn't alone.

The scene was typical of a protest in Charlottesville. About 60-70 people, most of them White, a few of them Black, majority all speaking up about the need for social justice, equity, and equality. The media was there, and in my mind, I was thinking that this was a good turn out and that the NAACP and others had did a good job at rallying up support. Little to my knowledge there was a short guy who was waiting in the wing for his opportunity to cause a scene. He was enraged by the turn that our city was taking. He hated the fact that we people of color, specifically black people who were taking bold steps to receive equity in our community. He was not the only one upset about a young black man being at the forefront of this change, but his bark was the loudest.

64

This was the same man who volunteered and worked on the President Obama Presidential campaign, whom decided that on this day he would make his voice heard.

His name was Jason Kessler, and he had been waiting in the shadows for an opportunity to get some attention. To my recollection, things at the protest were peaceful. People had signs, slogans were said, and I was about to leave. That was when Kessler decided to make his stance and his position heard. He burst out of the restaurant with a plate of Pasta in hand and few slogans of his own describing Black Lives Matter as Anti-White, how the NAACP was a fascist organization, and we all were there denying Doug Muir to his fundamental right to Free Speech. I had become use to the opposition and people attempting to be openly defiant, but most of the others in the crowd had not. Their initial response was to confront Kessler immediately, and that's exactly what he wanted. The media also rushed to Kessler to create a scene of chaos, which also played right into his hand.

I left shortly thereafter, but for the next couple of days I thought to myself that this was the beginning of something else. It wasn't the Confederate people, it wasn't the covert racists, it was something new for our area. A boldness of hate that we had seen on the national level reminiscent of the words and actions during the campaign for "45" was actually touching down in our community. I thought to myself that there had to be more people like the guy who came to Bella's, but where were they? Jason Kessler and the people like him were

65

becoming emboldened by Trump during his presidency. The ideas and ideology of "Make America Great Again" was rooted in the idea and premise that America was better when it was least diverse, when White people were in clear control, and the days of yesteryear were the best that we had ever had.

There was too much talk about diversity happening and the people who were normally at the top of the food chain now had to share the pie, and in some cases were getting a smaller piece. This sent a lot of White people into a sense of panic. They wanted the old days back. Trump knew that, and he tapped into it. Kessler did the same. When he decided to come out at Bella's and have his own counter protest, he put himself in a different stratosphere. He was willing to stand up to the groups that pushed for equity and equality, and he was willing to be a voice for the Oppressors, not the oppressed. Some framed it as he was a defender of free speech at the time. I wonder what they think now?

It would take a little more than a month for me to figure out that this battle was still in the early phases, and that I would be the target. Thanksgiving 2016 was the first family holiday that my wife and I had the opportunity to spend together, and it was a break that I was very much so looking forward to. We went down to Atlanta to see my mother before joining her family for their family reunion in Augusta, GA. It was finally some down time, or so I thought. Shortly after arriving, I started receiving phone calls from private phone numbers saying all kinds

of things. "Hey Nigger boy, your time is almost up."
"Everyone thinks that you're so *this and that*, but we are
going to show them the truth. Just wait on it." Or one
their personal favorite… "President Trump is your
president now, so you and that other monkey are both
about to be out of office." Just to name a few of the
things that were said during these calls. I can't lie, I was
a little disturbed, especially considering that I was
surrounded by family. But I expected some of it since
Trump had just shocked the world and won the
nomination to become President of the United States.
What I didn't know was that the guy from Bella's had
been planning an all-out attack on my character, and was
preparing to try and push me out of the way.

City Council as a whole began receiving emails about a
blog post created by Kessler with several tweets from
when I was 22,23, and 24 years old. The tweets were so
homophobic, sexist, and flat out disrespectful that I
originally didn't think that I wrote them. I talked it over
with my wife, friends, and colleagues, because I didn't
know what to do. I was wondering why this guy was
coming after me, but then it all made sense. This was the
same play that most White Supremacists made
throughout history. Whenever you see a black leader on
the rise, or in a prominent position, the easiest thing to
do in order to bring him/her down is to find dirt on them
and attack their character. In the Blog post, Kessler
literally portrayed me as a bigoted, homophobic, and
abhorrent individual who was leading an effort to
remove a statue that he coveted, and was furthermore

67

changing the landscape of a community that was just fine. Kessler had literally gone through over 150,000 tweets (yes, I was on twitter when it first started, always used it to talk, laugh, and be immature with my friends) and believed he had the ammunition that he needed to get me removed from office. It would only be a matter of time before the media would get a hold of the blog posts, and my team and I decided that instead of going back and forth and trying to decipher which tweet(s) were authentic, and which ones were not, I would just take full responsibility for what was said.

Being young, homesick, narrow minded, and admittedly shallow was who I was when I moved to Charlottesville in 2009. Growing up in Atlanta, attending college at an HBCU in South Carolina, and then moving to Charlottesville was a complete culture shock, and my tweets reflected such. Over the years, this community helped groom me into a much more level headed, mature individual who would soon become a husband, father, and community leader. Part of it was simply the evolution and growth that takes place between the years of 21-30. Part of it was also that I had learned that people didn't have to look like me to be able to stand up and support the same issues that I did. And the other part was that I just had a different outlook on life due to the fact that I was constantly around people who challenged me to grow in ways that I never had before.

Now, I was at a point in my life where I was comfortable with learning and growing. Unfortunately for many who read Kessler's blog post, those things were not what they saw. So, after spending a Thanksgiving holiday in crisis mode, giving a speech in front of family and friends in Atlantic Beach, South Carolina, and giving a talk at the White House, I returned to Charlottesville to face the music. It was a tough time for sure, but the stage was now set. It wasn't about a statue, it was about race, power, and the desire to either keep things the same or push to try and change them. Kessler had made his play, and now it was time to see how I would respond.

Chapter 11

A New Focus

Looking back to the week that followed Kesler's attacks... the emotions and experiences of those 7 days all fade together in a feverish blur. The City Council meeting that week was a zoo. Media outlets from across the country covered the story of the Vice Mayor whose horrible tweets were uncovered. And during one of the many phone calls I received that week during Thanksgiving, a person actually said to me that they were going "to take away everything that I loved, and break me down to a bare bone nigger with nothing to claim." And for a while, they tried. I also ended up resigning from the State Board of Education that week – thinking it in the best interest of the students of whom looked up to me and of so many in a community that felt like I had let them down. I remember thinking to myself that all of the things that I had worked so hard for were evaporating right before my eyes...

Truth be told, that week was probably one of the most chaotic times of my entire life. It was essentially like something out of a movie. However, this wasn't a script on the television, this was my real life. I was receiving backlash from throughout the city, throughout the state, and even more shocking, articles about my old tweets were being written about in the Washington Post and even talked about in news outlets in California. I remember thinking to myself that this couldn't be reality. Didn't everyone see that this was a ploy by a guy who was obviously trying to put a hit out on me to have me destroyed?

I was the same person that gave away hundreds of turkeys for Thanksgiving, the same man that gave away hundreds of coats at my annual Holiday giveaway, the same man that literally gave his energy, blood, sweat, and tears to the fight to make our area a better place. When people needed a job, I normally got the call. When there was a young man who needed a mentor, I would normally go and visit, and when there was a need for a person to step up, I did my best to be there. In my own pity and sorrow, I was forced to deal with the reality of the situation... this was bigger than me.

I went to the Westhaven Nursing Clinic to try and seek some wise council from one of my mentors and hero's, Dr. Holly Edwards – The last African American city councilor before I was elected, and the matriarch of our community. She was there with my other Auntie, Joy Johnson – A community activist who's been one of the leading voices in public housing redevelopment and a fierce advocate for the low-income community in Charlottesville. When I walked in, she didn't say a word, she just hugged me. She asked me if I was okay and told me that things would be alright. She said;

"You know, this is all part of God's plan. The stuff that they are trying to do to you is what they have always done. Don't worry baby, it's going to be ok."

Those words hit me to the core. I needed to hear them. I then walked into the back to see Mrs. Holly. She began to cry, and so did I. She said to me;

"They're trying to send a message to all of us. Don't get too high. Don't try for more. The moment that you do, we will bring you back down and put you in your place."

A tear fell down my face. She was right. But then she continued with a few words that I will never forget…

"You are going to beat this. As God is my witness, you will overcome this rough patch. Just keep your head high. Don't let them win. We got your back."

I think it was at that moment that I began to see that the worst week of my life, was actually all a part of the maturation process. Looking back, it was all divine. And I knew that it would take a spiritual village to pour back into me and bring me through. So, I spent my time crying and sobbing with my "other pastor" Dr. Alvin Edwards, pastor of Mt. Zion African Baptist Church, who uplifted me in return. I then spent time being empowered and ministered to by my brother Pastor Hodari Hamilton, who gave me words of encouragement and strength. God also sent me an angel in the form of a little Jewish

73

woman named Elly Tucker. Though I had never met her before, Pastor Edwards believed that she would be great to talk to, and he was right.

You see, my tweets were absolutely abhorrent and described a young man who was sexist, homophobic, narrow minded, and seemed to think that everything on twitter was funny. That much was true. I was ashamed of the tweets and disappointed in myself but I was also disappointed that even some of the people who had known me back then were also turning their backs. They were disregarding all of the positive work that I had done while growing up in my mid to late twenties and were only focused on the crazy things that I had done while young. It was like I was the bad guy, and that wasn't the truth. Elly seemed to get that though. Not once did she judge me, she just hugged me. Not one time did she try to make me feel bad for what happened, she simply spoke words of encouragement to me. It was hectic, but also a revealing time of seeing who my real friends were.

I still had city meetings to attend, still went to eat at restaurants where some people looked over me with disdain or up and down, with disgust, and there were others that smiled instead and gave me a hug. On one such occasion, I was eating dinner at Mel's diner with my daughters, trying to clear my head, and I got a phone call from Mark Brown. Mark was the owner of a local taxi company, owned a good bit of our downtown mall, owned the parking garages, and had a personality that caused people to either love him or hate him.

74

Not much older than I, Mark had helped me with my campaign to get on City Council. At the time he and I were bumping heads as the city was involved in a heated situation with Mark regarding his parking garages – and the people weren't cutting him any slack. As a councilman, it was my duty to put the city before a friendship, so, needless to say things were a little rocky between us for a while. We hadn't spoken in months, and now there he was out of the blue reaching out.

"Where are you?" He asked urgently. "I don't care where you are, I'm coming over right now." Mark had his own ways about him, but if he's in your corner, he's in your corner. So, although we had our differences, I knew from the tone of his voice that it meant he was serious and that he was, without a doubt, going to be here for me.

We talked outside of Mel's for a while, catching up before he gave it to me straight. "You gave the Confederates what they wanted on a silver platter. They've been trying to find a way to paint you as a racist asshole, and now these tweets give them all of the ammo that they need to try and bury you. *This is bad Wes.* Like really bad. White people aren't too happy with you right now. This is bad."

This was the harsh, kind of straight, tough love that Mark often gave. "But you know what, if you play this right, you will be okay. You can come back from it. It's a valuable lesson for you. Not everyone is your friend, and people in the shadows will come out of nowhere to trip you up. This will be a test of your character, and I think that you can handle it. Hold your head high. Eat a little bit of this humble pie, you need it, but then pick your head back up." He was right. I needed more than a slice of humble pie, however, I needed the whole pie and now I had to eat it.

It was clear, this statue situation wasn't what was fueling this. My tweets weren't what was fueling this. It was the fact that change was occurring and some people would do everything in their power to stop that change from happening. My wife, who had only been married to me for four and a half months now had to watch her superman be broken down, and figure out a way to help him back up. I was on the front page of the paper every day, and not in a good way. You couldn't turn on the news without seeing something negative. But she held on. I had never cried in front of my wife, but through it all she saw my tears, my fears, and she helped me regain my strength. Her coworkers were also great, as they made her feel not only welcomed at the new school she taught at, but they helped her deal with the things that I couldn't. There was a major shift happening however, and people were getting tired of the attacks. My students at Albemarle High School were starting petitions for me to come back to the school. The people in our new neighborhood provided us with love and support in spite of. The city overall, was showing me that while I may have resigned from the State Board of Education, that everything was going to be okay. They were still with me.

Slowly but surely, the love started to ignite like a wildfire. My colleagues provided statements in the media that they didn't believe my old tweets reflected who I was.

"Those past tweets were troubling, but they do not match my experience of the man today," Councilor Kathy Galvin said. "We respect each other and work hard for the good of the city. That's what matters now."

"Those of us who have known Mr. Bellamy since he moved to Charlottesville have seen him grow up before our eyes to be a remarkable young man," Councilor Kristin Szakos said. "Charlottesville is a city of second chances, and if anyone deserves one, it is Wes Bellamy. He does a lot of good for this community, and I support him wholeheartedly."

"Words don't bother me," said Councilor Bob Fenwick, adding that he thought it was a "shame that people who seem to want to find fault with someone have to keep digging until they find something. ...I think that's an issue we have to deal with nationally, as well as locally."

"If for one minute I thought Wes was going to walk out the door, I'd block it. That's what I think of him," Fenwick said. "He's a smart, energetic young man, and I'm glad I'm working with him on the council."

Now, Mike Signer, our mayor... not so much. Of all of my colleagues, Signer was the one who said in a statement "Bellamy should consider whether it is appropriate for him to stay in office or remain as Vice Mayor." He said that "in a time when we so urgently need unity, tolerance, and love" such communications "have done real harm to our community."

He went on to say, "I believe Mr. Bellamy must seriously consider how and whether, in his present role as Vice Mayor and as a city councilor, he can best serve the common good of Charlottesville... I can only say I will continue to work with all members of the council to bring tolerance and compassion to our community both inside and outside our chambers."

It honestly felt like this was his opportunity to turn the tide on me, and he took advantage of it. His words hurt, but it was also a valuable lesson. When some people see blood in the water, they look to take you out. I figured at this point, I had two options: either crawl into a hole and hide or come out with my head held high. I went to the barbershop that weekend, and just sat with my friends. As black culture shows, one of the best places to take your early punches, discuss and prep for what's about to happen is at the Shop. It was literally my place to escape. Throughout the week, the guys at the shop called and texted, checked on me, joked on me, and one of them, my brother Ray, even invited me over his house to just take a load off... He bought up the tweets and poked fun at me. I laughed, we laughed. It was the first time durng that whole ordeal that I had found anything funny. All of these people helped me see that I was going to be okay. Yeah, it was tough in the moment, but they reminded me that I was built for this. I could take it. I was also seeing social media swell with support. Message after message, post after post, tweet after tweet, #ImWithWes.

...And that was an amazing feeling.

It was Sunday and the City Council meeting was on Monday morning. Although, I was coming off one of the most hectic weeks of my life, I was feeling optimistic thanks to the people who had poured into me.

My sister Shemica, who had been by my side and supported me through and through, sent me a link to the front cover of the Richmond Times Dispatch newspaper. I looked down in confusion before clicking on the link. The front page opened and read:

Sunday, Richmond Times Dispatch –
"What to do About Wes Bellamy's Tweets."

I was instantly nervous. Didn't want to scroll down, let alone read it. The RTD was arguably the biggest newspaper in the state... but I know that if Shemica had sent it to me, then it must have been important enough to read. So, I did... I was shocked. They urged people to give me a break. I couldn't believe it. This was a defining moment. I knew that there was a long road ahead, sure, but there was clearly a light at the end of the tunnel. I was also reminded by several elders in the community later that day that these are the kinds of things that often happen to black leaders when trying to create change. They try and attack our character first and then our position. I came back home that night and noticed the newspaper still on the table where I had left it prior... placed my hand on it and let out a sigh.

I may have been uncertain about so many things before but one thing was for certain...

The city of Charlottesville had my back.

That meeting on Monday was unlike any other I had ever experienced. People had signs, banners, posters, and even shirts supporting me. It felt good to know that the place that I attributed much of my growth as a man to, didn't desert or leave me when the going got tough. This is also the same meeting that Kessler decided that he would attend, speak at, walk up to the crowd playing wrestling music, and make a complete fool out of himself. He admittedly said afterwards that he wanted to entertain the crowd, but from my perspective, this wasn't a joke. It was clear, he was on a mission to have me removed and fulfill the prophecy of whoever it was that called me. A petition was formed, and Kessler literally sat outside on the Downtown Mall and other parts of the city with a petition in hand to obtain signatures to have me removed from office. We eventually went to court and it was determined that social media posts from several years ago before I was elected were not grounds to have me removed, but again, his stage was set.

What I would often read and see was a feeling that I was only allowed to remain on City Council because I was black. If this was a white person, then they would have been removed or forced to resign. Black people, and other people of color, in this country were allegedly "getting all of the privileges." Specifically, in our city, in the eyes of the trolls, I was a "Black Supremacist" (whatever that means), who had tricked a lot of white people into supporting me. There was an underlying theme in their messaging. Similar to Make America Great Again, these people wanted to make *our area* great again. It was better when it was white.

So, now we have to take a few things into account – It had now been nearly a year since the initial call for the removal of the statues. In this time, there had been a community wide appointed Blue Ribbon Commission on Race and Public Spaces that provided a litany of recommendations that included either transforming the parks with confederate statues or removing the statues, being more intentional with telling the full story of race within our community through new landmarks, new statues, budget allocations, and a variety of other things.

Also, I had a little bit more time on my hands to focus on local matters revolving around equity. I wrote a proposal that was presented in February 2017 called the "Equity Package." The Equity Package was a comprehensive effort through policy and budgetary decisions to help level the playing field in Charlottesville. While pushing

81

the effort to have the statues removed people would often say, "Moving the statues isn't going to change anything. We should focus on schools, on housing, on jobs, etc.." I agreed with most people when they made that argument, and now that I had a year under my belt to be able to study the budget and the process of how government worked, I thought about a way to be able to address the valid concern that people had. They were right, removing a statue would only be symbolic in the eyes of some, however, when one is able to combine a symbolic removal with the addition of a substantive measure, you have a method for success, and a potential game changer.

I began to think about what the major blocks of change would come from based off of what I had been hearing from the community and came up with a proposal to be debuted the same night that we, city council, were set to take a vote on the statues and the recommendations from the Blue Ribbon Commission.

The Equity Package Included:

Education:

Charlottesville Scholarship Program:

In honor of former mayors Rev. Dr. Alvin Edwards, Charles Barbour, Vice-Mayor Dr. Holly Edwards, and others who have served on this same city council, City Council will establish a $5,000-a-year scholarship through the Charlottesville Scholarship Program in their name for Charlottesville City Schools graduates to attend an Historically Black College or University (HBCU) of their choice.

GED Training and Course Assistance:

City Council will allocate up to $20,000 to work with the Charlottesville Housing Authority and the Adult Learning Program, to provide free GED training and cover the cost of the GED exams for residents of our Public Housing sites and work to seek assistance for at least 50% of the tuition to PVCC for these GED completers.

Course Curriculum in Local Schools

City Council will offer a grant of <u>$15,000</u> for the creation of an Ethnic Studies course to be taught in our local schools, focusing on the history of people of color in the City of Charlottesville, in conjunction with the Charlottesville City Schools. This course will comply with all Standards of Learning (SoL) guidelines and requirements, and will expose local students to the history, the difficulties, accomplishments, and impact of people of color in and around the City of Charlottesville.

Coordinator for Black Youth Achievement:

As initially proposed by the Charlottesville Youth Council, this new position (est. cost $100,000 including salary, benefits and program budget) will focus on a community-wide effort to close gaps in opportunity and achievement in education and employment, coordinate and inform the work of non-profit and other community partners, and work with young African-American residents of Charlottesville to develop leadership skills, academic excellence and workforce readiness. This position may be housed in the Office of Human Services, Human Rights or the City Manager.

Housing

Charlottesville City Council will prioritize the allocation of $2.5 million dollars over the next five years into the City's Capital Improvement Plan for redevelopment of our local Public Housing. City Council and lead staff will convene a Town Hall meeting to explain in detail the partnership between City Council, CRHA, and PHAR for the new CACF grant. The program will include a clear explanation to the public of:

- the process of the Affordable Housing Fund
- where the city currently stands in regards to affordable housing, and
- the current plan for increasing more affordable housing.

85

City Council tasks staff with conducting a series of meetings and public education workshops to inform neighbors and concerned organizations in the SIA area and involve them in its implementation, including explanations of form-based code and initiatives in the SIA, and using input from those participants to help ensure that development does not displace low-wealth communities in the SIA while increasing the stock of affordable and moderately priced housing.

.

City Council will continue to work with PHA or other partners to provide funding for Down Payment Assistance:http://piedmonthousingalliance.org/2016/0 3/14/home-buying-home-repair-assistance-funding-now-available-orangedaleprospect-neighborhood/

Workforce Training and Employment

Charlottesville City Council will prioritize workforce training for residents who live in the SIA to assist with upward mobility.

The City will continue to push the GO Initiative in low-wealth communities throughout the City.

The Black Youth Achievement director will help to staff Circle of Brotherhood and other targeted employment and training initiatives for young people of color

Jefferson School African American Heritage Center

Charlottesville City Council will provide a one-time grant of $950,000 to the Jefferson School African American Heritage Center to provide ten assistance for this staple of the Charlottesville Community, and to ensure the successful refinancing of the building that will ensure its long-term viability.

Dialogue on Race

Dr. Holly Edwards and several other community leaders were the visionaries, and driving forces behind the local Dialogue on Race in 2010, City Council will allocate $10,000 to the Human Rights Commission and task this group with prioritizing a second round of the Dialogue on Race to the Charlottesville Community.

Slave Auction Block

In agreeance with the Blue Ribbon Commission Report, Charlottesville City Council will allocate $50,000 for a design competition and reinterpretation of the current slave auction block.

Tonsler Park

In an effort to create equity throughout the city. It has been stated that as short as two years ago, in the City's Capital Improvement Plan, we the City Council, task staff to put up to $250,000 back into the CIP for the construction of a Field House at Tonsler Park.

My colleague Kristin and I weren't sure where we were going to get the third vote to remove the statue from since our Mayor, Mike Signer was adamant that he believed the statue should remain in place, and my fellow councilor Kathy Galvin, who also believed that the statue should stay and we should transform the parks into something else. There was one wild card though – Councilman Bob Fenwick. Bob had attended every Blue Ribbon Commission meeting, and had told me on several occasions that he wasn't sure which way he would vote. One thing he was sure that we wanted though was more money in the budget for programs to help people in need and for parks like Tonsler Park.

I showed Bob my Equity Package, and he seemed impressed but he didn't truly believe that I could get it through the budget. The city council meeting was packed to the brim with people with a variety of opinions, and emotions were high. I remember the people with signs, people with posters and a lot more color in the room than normal. The actual vote to remove the statue was something unlike anything that I had ever been a part of or had bore witness too. Each councilor said their peace, with Kathy and Mike voting for the statue to stay, and Kristin and I voting to have them removed. Bob Fenwick abstained, which sent the room into a complete frenzy.

People who I had known for years, who were normally mild mannered or very calm, erupted with anger and disappointment. There was one quote that rang out, and to this day, still hits me in my heart...

"Ya'll always talking about you want more public participation. You want to hear from different voices. And when we actually come and voice our opinion, your minds were already made up. Ya'll don't want to hear us, ya'll want this town to be the same old shit that it's always been. I'll never come to another city council meeting, because ya'll don't care about us."

If I had ever heard anything, it was that. That was the feeling of so many of the people that I had begged to come to the meetings and allow their voices to be heard, that was the feeling of the people who decided to not come to the meetings because as they would say, as my elder and brother from the neighborhood had told me all that time ago:

"Them people going to do what they want to do anyway Wes. You only one person, This stuff been here for years. You ain't about to change nothing."

It was the feeling of defeat that I had heard about, but never wanted to truly believe. The scene was one of utter sadness and disappointment, but all was not lost. Shortly after that vote, I called the question of the vote of the Equity Package, which passed unanimously. We got the substance that a lot of people asked for, and it was enough to get Bob over the finish line. Two days later he called a special press conference on his own and announced that he would be voting to have the statues removed. Progress was being made. The first major battle in this proverbial war was won, but I would soon learn that this was a marathon, not a sprint.

By April of 2017, things were progressing, but the fight still continued. Jason Kessler was now focused solely on removing me from public office. He would literally go out in 30-degree weather with a clipboard soliciting signatures from people to file a petition to have me recalled from office. In my opinion, it was just a play out of the old playbook to do whatever was necessary to get the Black Vice Mayor out of office. In retrospect, I think back to his remarks about how he was going to come after all of the councilors who voted for the statue removal, but the only one who he took to court was me. Kessler was so focused on having me removed that he actually got into a physical altercation at the downtown mall with a patron because the person wouldn't adhere to his request of signing the petition to have me removed. While Kessler was running around with a petition, there was another gentleman by the name of Mason Pickett who would walk around the city with a board that read "Wes Bellamy is a Jackass." He could be seen at local parks, outside of administrative buildings, on visible highways and byways, and at other various locations throughout the city. It was interesting to say the least, and reminded me daily of just how much work *still* needed to be done. Again, this wasn't about a statue. Leading an effort to remove a statue does not make people act this way.

This was about more.

I had also analyzed more of the budget and saw that there was an opportunity for us to increase the amount of minority contracts that the city awarded by revamping the policy and hiring a couple of new staff positions. We were moving towards being a more equitable city in a variety of ways. Not by the loud and headline attention grabbing things, but the items with substance that created pathways to change the game over the long haul.

Chapter 12

The Tiki Torch Rally That Backfired

It was May 13th, 2017 - around 9:30 PM or so when everything hit the proverbial fan. I was on my on my way back to Charlottesville, mauling over my plans for the week in my head as I interacted with my children – nothing out of the ordinary for me, or at least that's what I thought. Suddenly, my phone started buzzing off the hook. So much so that my wife had to turn to me to ask what was wrong. Activists were calling and asking me if I had noticed anything different in the city. My wife, children and I had spent majority of the day out of town and we were just returning – so I had no idea what they were speaking about. Almost immediately, as we were entering onto Barracks road into Charlottesville, the energy shifted. It felt like a young flame igniting or a tension so tight that I could hardly breathe. It's hard to describe but I could literally sense that a lot of people were on edge. I for one, wasn't sure what was going on or what was bubbling at the surface but I knew in that moment, something was reading itself to explode.

More people started calling me and telling me to get to Emancipation Park as soon as possible, I knew something was up. In true millennial fashion, I went to check the first place to look when anyone starts getting calls like that – Twitter. I felt an instant rush of rage. It must have been visible because my wife began comforting me and all I could do was pass her the phone as I explained to her why she and the kids had to go home. When I got to the park, the damage had already been done. The news reports tell only part of the story...

From the Washington Post:

"Self-proclaimed white nationalist Richard Spencer led a large group of demonstrators carrying torches and chanting "You will not replace us" Saturday in Charlottesville, protesting plans to remove a Confederate monument that has played an outsize role in this year's race for Virginia governor...

"What brings us together is that we are white, we are a people, [and] we will not be replaced," Spencer said at an afternoon protest, the first of two rallies he led in the town where he once attended the University of Virginia.

At the second rally, dozens of torch-bearing protesters gathered in a city park Saturday evening and chanted "You will not replace us" and "Russia is our friend," local television footage captured. Spencer was not shown addressing that gathering, but he tweeted a photo of himself standing in the crowd carrying what appeared to be a bamboo tiki torch."

Let me tell you what they didn't say about that day however. This wasn't about a vote by City Council to remove a statue, this was about preserving Whiteness by any means necessary. People don't just attempt to recreate a scene reminiscent of the Klu Klux Klan over a statue of Robert E. Lee. Richard Spencer believed that what was *his* was being taken away. In his eyes, we were attempting to change the landscape of the entire area.

So, let's put that into context. What the nation saw that night in May was nearly 40 white men in white shirts enter our city earlier in the day, not that night. Every year Charlottesville hosts a festival called the "Festival of Culture" an event that brings together a wide variety of people all whom have displays, food, and culturally significant wares for sale whilst having fun celebrating our differences. It's a kid friendly event, and one that a lot of people look forward to. What was different about 2017 was that the event also had a new set of visitors. A lot of White Men dressed like some stock photo in a modern-day White Supremacy magazine. Their uniform was one that was consistent with their "modern" message. White tops and Khaki pants. They paraded around the downtown area not overtly looking to intimidate, but more or less looking to make their presence known. I had received a couple of phone calls about them earlier in the day, but honestly thought little of it. I thought it was just a group of cowards looking to get a reaction. In fact, what they were doing was setting the stage for their later display. This was about intimidation. This was about trying to show that they were going to fight for their belief that our community, our city, our state should return to the days in which White men ruled the land and made the decisions. Again, this was not about a statue. When Spencer leads a chance that says "You will not replace us." the meaning is deeper than what appears at the surface. Right after the tiki torch rally, people were still in denial. "This isn't Charlottesville." In fact, initially, I was one of those people. However, in retrospect, I was wrong. That Tiki Torch rally *was* Charlottesville. Spencer attended the University of Virginia. You know who else was at the rally that night? Jason Kessler, also a graduate of the University of Virginia. In the eyes of many, there is no Charlottesville without UVA. These people felt right at home. They were there that night to recreate an image of the past and invoke fear into a community as an intimidation tactic, just like their forefathers who rode around on horses with burning crosses did in decades before. The goal was simple. Scare as many people as possible. Show the nation and more importantly for them, the internet, that they were unafraid and were willing to stand up for their belief that White was right. That tiki torch rally was for every "liberal", every person of color, every person who believed in "diversity", and was also intended to scare the "Black Supremacist-Extremist" who was the Vice-Mayor at the time. In their eyes, I started all of this, and their belief was that this gesture would scare me away, and it would be finished. Later that evening, a group of them rode up and down my neighborhood, one of the last remaining predominately African American neighborhoods in the city, yelling out a few slurs in another method to scare us. I laugh about it sometimes because I honestly don't know what the hell would make them think that some tiki torches, a couple of clowns full of liquid courage, and some "tough tweets" and social media posts would scare me away. I, like many others were pissed. They made a move. It was cute. But they underestimated a couple of things. This wasn't the movies or a White Supremacist fairy tale. You don't just do something stupid, and scare the Black man and his friends/family away. Nah. It doesn't work that way.

That night, I said a few things on twitter about it. Acknowledged that we saw their little act, but we weren't afraid. I called on our Commonwealth Attorney, Dave Chapman to bring about charges on those in attendance. As stated in the Daily Progress: "City Councilor Wes Bellamy called for the ralliers to be prosecuted. He cited section 18.2-423.01 of the Virginia Code, which states that "any person who, with the intent of intimidating any person or group of persons, burns an object on a highway or other public place in a manner having a direct tendency to place another person in reasonable fear or apprehension of death or bodily injury is guilty of a Class 6 felony."

"When White Supremacists Make odes to White Power, and clearly use torches to send a message to our community that they are the superior race while trying to strike fear and intimidate others, they are breaking the law," Bellamy wrote on Facebook.

City police said in a statement that the department was conferring with local officials about possible legal action." According to one of the most respected local attorneys in the area, the statute that I was referencing did not apply. The statute, § 18.2-423.01. Burning object on property of another or a highway or other public place with intent to intimidate; penalty.

A. Any person who, with the intent of intimidating any person or group of persons, burns an object on the private property of another without permission, is guilty of a Class 6 felony.

B. Any person who, with the intent of intimidating any person or group of persons, burns an object on a highway or other public place in a manner having a direct tendency to place another person in reasonable fear or apprehension of death or bodily injury is guilty of a Class 6 felony.

While subsection (B) might seem applicable to a Nazi torch-lit parade, the United States Supreme Court has made it quite clear that Richard Spencer and his friends can't be prosecuted under this statute.

Our Commonwealth Attorney eventually declined to pursue charges, stating that he believed the aforementioned statute was too narrow and would be difficult to prove in court. In my opinion, I disagreed, as did several attorneys, and furthermore this decision empowered the White Supremacists even more. It made them believe, to a certain extent, that they were above the law. They had found a way to make the laws work to their advantage. *Hmmmm*. White Supremacists and people dressed in all white with torches using the law to their advantage to invoke fear seems a little... familiar.

But I digress.

The Tiki Torch Rally that had maybe 100 people show up to spew hate, actually inspired a community led vigil the next night that had nearly 500 people in attendance. Led by activists' groups including our local Black Lives Matter chapter, Showing up for Racial Justice (SURJ), APOC, and others, a massive showing of love, resistance, and togetherness came about. It was one more step in our community coming together to show that we were stronger than those attempting to take over. We were also coming to grips with the fact that we were in a fight with an evil group of people who were hell bent on sending us back to the days of yesteryear. The choice that we all had to make was clear. We have to stick together. What sticking together actually looks like, was something different.

In the days after, Tiki Torch Rally and the subsequent counter rally of unity the next day, the city was on edge. There were mixed emotions to say the

101

least. While the White Supremacists decided to come with nearly 100 clowns dressed in white and yield tiki torches, there was a strong push back of nearly 500 people in the same park pushing back. Even with our strong showing, there were still some people who were scared, some people were upset, others were dumbfounded and wondered why the police who were there just sat and watched those with tiki torches, why the commonwealth attorney refused to go after the patrons, and why couldn't city council stop them from coming back. To a certain extent, those three themes would be the themes throughout the summer. We didn't do nearly enough. We weren't proactive enough. We fought back, but not in the ways that we should have. But in the midst of all of this, some good was coming. I was noticing a community of people who were waking up. A lot of White people were now coming to realize just how the statue of Robert E. Lee was being used as a ploy to push the agenda of White Supremacy. I was seeing a lot of people say things that they refused to say months earlier. If you thought that statue needed to stay, then essentially you were on the side of Richard Spencer. Jason Kessler and his minions were not there to defend the statue, they were there to defend their whiteness.

People were finally starting to see what many of us were saying the entire time. However, while the mood was changing throughout the city, my mayor, Mike Signer was steadfast in his belief that the statue should stay. This provided more tension on the council, as I took a clear position. If you can't come along after basically a reenactment of the 1924 KKK, then you never will understand our perspective. Also, let me be clear, by *our*, I mean Black People, people of color, and all of those in the city who clearly saw what was going on. However, this was also a memorable point in all of this. There was still a contingent of people in the city and the county who believed that Spencer, Kessler, and the many other White racists were utilizing their free speech, didn't break any laws, and we should just ignore them. It almost felt as if people were doing everything in their power to not acknowledge that we had a problem within our community. The topic of race had grabbed the attention of everyone in our community, but yet, some still believed that things were not "that bad..."

Well we were all about to see, that things could actually get worse.

Chapter 13

The KKK Rally and Wedding Milestones

The summer was approaching, and the mood in the city was one of uncertainty. There was talk that Jason Kessler was planning a follow-up of the Tiki Torch rally – touting it as one of the biggest rallies that the "Right" will have ever seen. In my mind, this was cause for concern. The climate in the country since 45 had become president was one that emboldened a lot of closeted racists and empowered those who were already proud white supremacists. As an elected official, I was thinking about ensuring that we kept the community safe, but also wondering what was going to happen. People were affirming my concerns by coming to the city council meetings and hitting me up on Twitter and other social media outlets saying that the Kessler rally was going to be tough. People were saying that they had heard things that we all should take very seriously. This was not an event to take lightly.

Around the same time, we were also informed that the Klu Klux Klan from North Carolina wanted to come to

Charlottesville on July 8th to protest as well. There was an instant fit of rage that flowed through me upon hearing that not one, but two separate hate groups wanted to come to our town to stir up trouble. I had thoughts about wanting to fight back, but also thoughts of keeping my people safe. I also understood how enraged by the thought of the Klan coming to our city our people must be and how they would want to retaliate.

As a husband, July 8th was a prominent date for me- it was my one-year wedding anniversary. The year had been a tough year, but my wife and I made it in spite of our difficulties. Considering that our entire world had been turned upside down, I was pleased to say that this was not a small feat. It was one that deserved to be celebrated, so we made plans to go to a place that my wife had always wanted to go to – New York City. Things were all set; the tickets were purchased and we were ready and excited to go. But here we were, in early June hearing that the Klu Klux Klan was coming to Charlottesville. Thankfully, over the course of the year, I had developed a much thicker skin. I learned to expect the unexpected. I learned that when things seemed to be the calmest, the storm was on the horizon. They had chosen that date - July 8th, 2017. The same day as my wedding anniversary, which wouldn't have been hard to find online. This was not coincidence. This was a clear message.

While being briefed about the KKK coming to town there was another message passed along to me, "Wes, Kessler is also planning a rally called Unite the Right, the month after the KKK rally." Clearly, now was not the time to play around because these hate groups weren't playing around either. The community was in a frenzy about the Klan coming. However, one thing that I found refreshing was the amount of people who were unafraid in the face of impending conflict, but who were instead, speaking up within the community about how to handle the situation.

We held community meetings in churches and barbershops, within the neighborhoods, and everywhere else who would hear us. A lot of black people were saying that we shouldn't show up, arguing that the White Supremacists wanted us to come down there, confront them, so that we would be the ones going to jail for hurting them. Others felt that we had an obligation to confront the Klan and let them know that they weren't welcomed in our city. I was on the fence, between both sides, about what our approach should be. What I did know, however, was that if I went there, I would be an instant lightening rod, and to a certain extent an open target. My wife had specifically asked me not to go. She wanted for us to have at least one special day that was just for us. Not for the movement, not for Charlottesville, not for anyone or anything else except for us. I prayed on it, and decided that she was right. We traveled to New York, and I received consistent updates from both the City Manager and my folks on the ground. The day of the actual event, I woke up in Manhattan with my wife. I promised her to give her as much of my attention as she wanted on our special day, and she told me that she understood that I would be checking in on what was happening back in Charlottesville. I hadn't really been super vocal about the fact that I wasn't going to be in Charlottesville on July 8th, for a variety of reasons:

1) I didn't want those who intended to do myself, and my family harm to have easy access to my whereabouts.

2) I didn't think it was necessary, which in hindsight, may have been a mistake. At the KKK rally, it appeared that only 30 members of the Klu Klux Klowns from North Carolina showed up. Some with signs, some with weapons, others with only fear. The city definitely showed up and showed out. Nearly 500 people with horns, instruments, loud pipes, posters, and the energy and love that showed that we were stronger than the KKK was present. In addition, there were events spread out throughout the city for everyone who chose to not confront the KKK but still wanted their voice to be heard.

The tell-tale sign for the city that we were in a time of revolution was that the counter protest at the park outweighed everything else that was going on in the city. To me, this proved that people wanted to confront the evil, and to let them know that they weren't welcome. We could have all the discussions about not meeting fire with fire that we wanted. The fact remained that people had a right to be able to let these cowards know that they were not welcome in our city. They didn't have to ignore them, for that could have been seen as allowing these people to actually normalize their behavior. Some will

108

say that the confrontation is exactly what they wanted, and those who confront them are playing into their hand. Everyone, of course, is entitled to their own opinion, but, it's much more important for these clowns to know that whenever and wherever they decide to be in Charlottesville, someone will also be there to let them know that they aren't welcome.

The day as a whole was tough. It began with confrontation and a few activists briefly going to jail for blocking the pathway of the KKK as they tried to come in. It was obvious that the KKK members were terrified, and they tried to scurry out of the park as soon as they could. During the rally, I began to get messages and pictures from people on the ground. While it appeared that the KKK was frightened, they had the courage to hold signs with my name on it that read: "Wes Bellamy, go be a Nig somewhere else." Now think about it- if they were there to protest the removal of the statue, why the hell would one of them write such a thing? It's obvious that this was never about a statue.

As the rally came to an end, a few activists were still voicing their opinions about the event, the police, and the environment overall. These activists were tear-gassed. This was unacceptable, and it set the tone for the summer. While a lot of people were pleased with their blatant defiance and showing up the KKK, others were beginning to see a different picture. The narrative of the community versus the police vs the White supremacists was brewing. Whether the narrative was valid or not was unimportant. Unfortunately, perception is reality, and when unarmed activists are arrested, treated harshly, and tear gassed, while the KKK are protected and escorted out of the area, we have an issue. Yes, I am well aware that the protest was "peaceful" in the eyes of the law, but that did not negate the fact that their mere presence nearly incited a riot. To add to this, they were gassed, the perception that the police was not on the side of the community and activists was a real thing. It mattered little why it happened.

The fact remained, people were gassed after the KKK had left, and the people who came here to invoke terror via intimidation with their white robes, sent a bad message to the community. Simultaneously, I was getting notifications from a lot of people saying that I should have been at the rally. Essentially, some of it was "Wes you started all of this and you didn't even show up?" While I was not about to put the KKK, or any protest, before my wife, a new narrative was also being brewed:

Wes doesn't have our back.

It was a crazy time in Charlottesville, and while we should have been coming together before one of the disrespectful events of our time was on our horizon, many of us were at odds. Like Jay-Z said "It was the best of times, but it was the worst of times." Best of times because the city showed that it would stand up to hate, but worst because we were still at odds with each other, and that is what the white supremacists wanted.

The days following the KKK rally set the tone for the upcoming Unite the Right Rally. People were livid that they were tear gassed by the same people who had sworn to protect and serve them. To make matters worse, Gary Pleasants, the Deputy Police Chief at the time, came out and stated that he gave the call, not our chief of police, Al Thomas, to gas the protestors. Furthermore, he blamed the protestors for being gassed, saying in an interview,

"It's terrible for this community, but people brought this on us," he said. "A lot of people not from around here brought this on, and some people locally did it, and we have to deal with it."

Pleasants didn't have the best reputation amongst many in the community, and when he came out and blamed the protestors for what had occurred, it sent a bad message. He later went on to say, almost bragging, that he made the decision to deploy the tear gas on the protesters. It also didn't help that people had evidence that the police were being cozy with a well-documented white supremacist, Jason Kessler. Also, on the evening of July 8th after everything had settled down, our mayor at the time, Mike Signer put out a statement on Facebook that upset many people.

It read:

"At the end of the day, our Police succeeded in executing their strategy of protecting both the First Amendment and public safety up to and during the KKK rally. The rally concluded in less than an hour. After the rally concluded there was a disturbance during which protesters apparently released pepper spray and officers released three canisters of tear gas. Despite this unfortunate event, and the fact that over 1000 people were in attendance, many armed, only 2 people were treated for heat injuries and one for an alcohol-related issue. There were 23 arrests...

All in all, I believe that we came out of this difficult day stronger than before -- more committed to diversity, to racial and social justice, to telling the truth about our history, and to unity. On a hot day, we made lemonade out of a lemon - from North Carolina, no less."

While I had been speaking with a lot of different people during the event, it was nothing compared to what I saw and heard when I got back. I was initially told that things were fine, and for the most part peaceful. That was not the case. In an effort to keep my sanity and peace, I like to play basketball and lift weights with friends a couple days out of the week around 6 AM. I also enjoy jogging around the city to kind of feel the pulse of the city on the ground and see or hear from people who I normally don't interact with. I went for a jog that Monday, and I was literally stopped no less than 10 times by people saying

112

that they had a negative experience at the rally. Some of this was to be expected, but I was a little concerned with the frequency of it all. I also got a few phone calls from guys that I hoop with who told me about their experience during the KKK rally. I thought this too was a little strange considering the people who were calling were normally mild mannered and for the most part people who had favorable opinions about the police. The last thing that really showed me that something went awry at the rally was a call and text message that I received from a close confidant who I affectionately called "Unc."

Unc is an older Jewish man in his 70s, who is respectable, non-confrontational, and level headed. What he told me absolutely startled me. He described how he saw law enforcement officers being downright disrespectful, heavy handed, and rude to the counter protestors. Something wasn't right about all of this. Throughout the week, more and more were coming out and people were upset.

There's always more than one side to every story of course, so I sat out to speak with a few of our local law enforcement officers to get their perspective on what happened. From what I gathered, it was a hostile situation, and a lot of our officers believed that they were in a tough spot. Chief Thomas and I were close at the time, and we had a couple of conversations about what happened, and I tried my best to understand his viewpoint. Things were getting out of hand, people were being asked repeatedly to disburse and settle down, some officers believed that they were in danger, so the gas was deployed. I didn't quite agree with this assessment since it really didn't mesh with what most of the people that I was speaking with had said, but I wasn't there, so I had to try my best to weigh it all. Whether I was at church, jogging, at the park, or even at the grocery store, people were asking me;

"Wes, why did the police act like that?
How can ya'll protect the KKK, but not protect us?"

Repeatedly, people were saying that the Klu Klux Klan received better treatment than the people who lived in our community. Now while I believed that was a little farfetched, I could understand their perspective. I heard it best while listening to a debate about the KKK rally at the barbershop. A couple brothers said that they didn't go because they knew they would have been mad and would have attempted to hurt the KKK. A couple others said they went, and were left just as upset because they had lived in Charlottesville their entire life and had never seen the police protect them in their neighborhoods the way that they protected the KKK. They felt betrayed and overall, it reinforced a belief that the police, the system, and the powers that be were not here to ensure our safety. The idea of "Protect and Serve" didn't apply to the poor, to the disenfranchised, and it definitely didn't apply to the Black. I will admit, I was conflicted. I had come to know a lot of police officers since I had been in office. Some of us played basketball together and I got to know the people behind the badge. I knew that most of them were good people, so for the life of me, I couldn't understand what happened. I wanted to have faith in them, because I knew the chief and most of the ranking officers. I knew that they were trying to be better and work to be the change that our community wanted to see. The problem was that the community didn't feel this way and were calling for action. I was in a tough spot and our next city council meeting was quickly approaching. Something had to be said, and something had to be done. The first city council meeting after the KKK rally on July 8th was heartbreaking. We heard some of the most passionate speeches ever spoken by people who were tired, frustrated, and truly hurt by what transpired. During the meeting I called for the City Manager to follow up on the demands from the Legal Aid Justice Center asking for a report on what happened on July 8th. I later took to Facebook to post the following:

"Tonight, at the city council meeting, we heard from residents of the city, and nearby areas about their experiences at the July 8th KKK rally. While we have received literally, hundreds of emails, I must admit, the personal stories told tonight, the passion, the hurt, the pain, and the tone of it all really struck my spirit. I completely and earnestly agree with the speakers who spoke about how morality and law are not one and the same. In fact, historically, laws were put in place to specifically keep people who look like me from having the same liberties as others. As one of the speakers forcefully stated, we, specifically African Americans, are always told to "ignore", to "be silent", to "look the other

115

away", or some other variation of not speaking up and speaking out.

I want to be clear, as I stated tonight at the council meeting, I absolutely love Chief Thomas and our Charlottesville Police Department. I think the Chief is doing a great job, but that does not mean that our community does not deserve an answer about how they believe they were treated on July 8th. I also want everyone to understand that there is nothing wrong with being passionate and/or expressing your frustration about how you feel. Personally, I would like for us to use that energy to address economic, educational, and housing inequities, mentor a youth, or serve on a commission or board, but people DO have the fundamental right to express themselves as they choose.

I know first-hand what it feels like to be beaten up by law enforcement, to be pulled over, thrown out of my car, have drug dogs called, and told "Nigger never come back around these parts." Trust me, I fully understand the feeling of being treated unfairly by people who wear a badge. However, I've also spoken with several members of local Law Enforcement who expressed the feeling of frustration of having people call them "KKK lovers" have items thrown at them, and spat on for doing their jobs. In NO way shape, form, or fashion is this ok. The police aren't our enemies, and for the most part, they deserve our respect and support, but that does not negate the fact that our community deserves answers for what they believed they experienced on July 8th. My aunt would tell me all of the time, "If you didn't do anything wrong, then you don't have anything to worry about... so let me check and see."

For the sake of transparency, I agree with the Legal Aid Justice Center, and I am calling on our City Manager, Police Chief, and City Staff to address the following:

ii) acknowledge that the deliberate choice to use warzone tactics on July 8th—instead of planning for de-escalation—is inconsistent with Charlottesville's values and good policing;

ii ii) authorize and initiate an independent investigation into law enforcement's actions before, during and after the permitted demonstration on July 8th to determine whether any actions were unlawful; and

iii iii) ensure accountability for any unlawful tactics used, whether by the Charlottesville Police Department (CPD) or the Virginia State Police (VSP).

Furthermore, also address the following actions requested by Legal Aid: We call on the City Council to take the following steps to investigate the events of July 8th and prepare for August 12 "Unite the Right" rally:

1. Authorize and initiate an independent investigation of the events of July 8th, including allegations of violence by law enforcement against civilians. Such an investigation

117

should not be conducted by those local or state agencies participating in the law enforcement response on that day, should include multiple opportunities for public input, and should further address such topics as:

A. Why/Who requested the Virginia State Police? On what terms were they requested? What conversation was there about the show of force requested?

B. Whose police officers were dressed in riot gear and why were those officers sent to the area?

C. Who declared Saturday's counter protest an "unlawful assembly," and why? What factors about the counter protest warranted this declaration?

D. Who ordered the deployment of tear gas and what was the reason for that decision?

2. Pass a resolution calling on law enforcement to plan for de-escalation of tension and the least aggressive means for maintaining safety at the August 12th "Unite the Right" rally. Flowing from this resolution should be a clearly articulated plan for August 12th that protects the rights of counter-demonstrators and provides detailed de-escalation procedures for law enforcement.

3. Enact, as policy, a requirement that any law enforcement agency asked to assist CPD in carrying out its responsibilities agree to abide by CPD rules of engagement.

4. Appoint an advisory committee, made up of community stakeholders, advocates, civil rights experts, de-escalation experts, law enforcement officials, and governmental leaders, to work with the City Council, the CPD and other law enforcement agencies that might be called upon to assist before August 12th to ensure that the civil liberties of all participants and protesters are protected (Only if we believe that our current Citizens/Police Advisory Panel does not suffice).

5. Set conditions on the use of private security personnel by any individuals or groups seeking permits to use public facilities that ensure that the role of such personnel is carefully delineated and the scope of their authority is understood by them and by CPD and carefully and effectively communicated to the public.

6. Establish a permanent Civilian Review Board for the Charlottesville Police Department comprised of city residents, advocates, and other community members. This board should have the authority to, among other actions, investigate complaints against law enforcement; hire independent prosecutors to pursue charges; and make binding recommendations for disciplinary action where warranted.

119

We call on the Charlottesville Police Department and I have a feeling in my chest that I have not had for some time. I feel like those whose shoulders we stand on are screaming. They are watching and waiting for us to do what is right. It feels like they want us to do all of the things that they couldn't do. And in this particular moment, it means for everyone to use their collective power and energy to stand up for what is right. At this moment and time, as an elected official in this city, I believe this to be right.

"#Empower #StandTall #Resist #NewCville"

This set off a chain reaction. While the public and the community were happy that I spoke up for them, the police felt as if I betrayed them. As a result of this, Chief Thomas and I would not chat for a couple of weeks. In theory, my thought was that if we didn't do anything wrong or have nothing to hide, then we should just complete a report and let the people know what happened. We should be able to simply say what happened, admit to mistakes, and devise a plan to move forward. Unfortunately, this isn't quite how the Chief and some of the police officers took my statement.

Apparently, they believed that I was calling for a Department of Justice investigation, and they needed to be prepared. While this back and forth was taking place, we were less than one month away from the Unite the Right rally.

It was like a cloud was hanging over the heads of us all, and we were trying our best to navigate it all. The activists in the community were clear that this was going to be bad, and we need to be prepared. Kessler appeared to be on a press tour and looking to rally all the troops that he could to fall into our city on August 11th to unleash their wrath on us. We soon got word that nationally and internationally known White Nationalists were scheduled to come to Charlottesville. The mood and energy in the city was a lot different from the weeks before the KKK rally. It was like we were looking to fight the unknown. When the KKK was coming, it was something familiar: A bunch of old white racists who were trying to hold on to the past, and were simply coming to try to "rile us up" as my grandmother would say. Yes, we knew that the group was from North Carolina, but we had pockets of the Klan close to us in greater Charlottesville. We also knew that it would be no more than 40 of them, that they would be severely outnumbered, and it would be a lot of people who wanted to come out and openly let them know that they were not welcome. It was an enemy, if you will, that we had seen before, that wasn't relevant, and we could defeat in a variety of ways. The Unite the Right rally presented a different challenge. The activist community had been scouring the internet and dark net for a while now, and they were adamant that the people coming here on August 11th and 12th were serious people who wanted to invoke pain, terror, and real violence. The problem was that we couldn't prove it. This was when I learned that common sense wasn't all that common. The growing sentiment throughout the community was that we should simply deny Kessler's request for a permit at Emancipation Park. He was acting as if he had a permit, when he didn't. Our legal advice was for the city council to not discuss the permit, as we had to review all options, and be as fair as possible.

For me it was simple. These people have committed violent acts in Portland, Berkeley, and other cities throughout the United States. I spoke to the mayor of Berkeley and other elected officials and to folks on the ground in Portland, and their message was one that was consistent. These folks are coming to fight, but it's difficult to do anything about it because they are going to come under the First Amendment and if you try to shut them down, they will claim that you are denying their first amendment right to free speech. You will be sued, and they will win. City council had several meetings with first amendment attorneys and experts who had opinions on what we could and couldn't do. We had to walk a fine line. Under no circumstance could we deny anyone's first amendment. People had the right to be able to express themselves and their political views as they saw fit, and they had the right to do so in public spaces. We were briefed by the state police and representatives from a variety of law enforcement offices, and it was stated to us that there had to be a credible threat for them to intervene in a method that would do what the community was calling for. While it appeared that the social media posts of people saying that they were going to come to Charlottesville and run people over, shoot me personally, or do all kinds of vile and inhumane things to our citizens and those who vowed to protect us seemed to be credible, it wasn't credible in the eyes of the law. It was all just things said on "social media…"

We, the city and city council, were in a tough predicament. People from all over the state were watching and asking what we were going to do, and we couldn't quite talk about it. We couldn't tell Kessler and his crew that they were not allowed to come to the city because that would violate their first amendment rights. It was also rather apparent that counter protestors from across the country would also be coming to Charlottesville to try to protect the people on the ground, and in their view, fight the good fight. Simultaneously, I was receiving Facebook messages, emails, and phone calls from different militia groups who were also planning to attend. There had also been a strong push from local clergy to bring in 1,000 clergy members from across the country to come and pray, to stand in solidarity with the city, and to let their voices be heard. I found the clergy members and local activists' positions really refreshing. I was really struggling with the lack of participation from some of our church leaders early on, and it was frustrating to say the least. However, things had shifted.

The clergy became more vocal and they showed their support in a variety of ways. They were getting into the fight, standing up, refusing to back down, and fulfilling their role. You see, in this, everyone has a role to play. From the elected officials, to the activists, to the students, to the parents, to the regular people in the community, we all have a role to play.

"DO SOMETHING."

It was rather simple in my eyes, either you were going to stand up and fight or you were going to stand idle and lay down. This was one of the pivotal and turning moments in our community, we HAD to stand up. We could not allow the hate to win. And while my blood was pumping as we got closer and closer, my wife was more on edge than ever before. She was incredibly nervous. We had thought the KKK was going to make me a target, and we saw their signs and propaganda which showed that they were there to rattle our city, and send a message, but they failed. However, that was only 50 people. This was going to be over 1,000 White Supremacists, many with guns, many with weapons, and she was terrified of what they may potentially try to do to me. She wasn't the only one.

There is a core group of about twenty black men in our community who consider themselves my protectors in one way or another. They often watch my house, they go with me to different places, and they work diligently to ensure that I am safe at all times. They were also nervous and prepared for the worst. I, on the other hand, was fully aware of the potential danger of the pretty big bullseye on my back, but to be honest, I wasn't really that worried about it. Maybe I was being naive, maybe I had a false sense of security, or maybe I was just ready to get it all over with, but all in all I wasn't really feeling an immense sense of danger. I had read a lot of the message boards, and saw that some of the white supremacist had put up pictures of my home and my address, or said that they were going to do different things to me. I had a wife and children in my home who I knew that I was willing to protect by any means necessary, but also on my mind was my dissertation defense, scheduled for 1:00 PM on Friday August 11th. God seemed to send me a healthy distraction to put my mind at ease. Leading up to the KKK rally in July, I had called for several community town halls, had a variety of clergy and community members involved in the pre-planning, and was on social media daily talking about different options for the day of the event, as well as why we shouldn't take the bait. I didn't really do any of that before the August 12th rally.

Part of it was that I was admittedly upset that some people blamed me, and not the KKK, for their coming to Charlottesville. Another part of it was that in the aftermath people had took to social media and said that I should have skipped my first wedding anniversary and went out and yelled at the Klu Klux Klan. The worse of it all was that they assumed that I didn't have a clear plan to tell anyone until maybe a few days before the event. But they were wrong.

For nearly a month I was working on fine tuning my dissertation and preparing for my defense at Virginia State University. For three days a week from July to August I drove the 90 miles to and from Charlottesville to Petersburg to meet with my dissertation chair, Dr. Silas Christian. He informed me that if I wanted to be Dr. Wes Bellamy, I needed to zero in and finish this as soon as possible. So, that's what I did. I attempted to block out the distractions, provide my input as much as possible, be there for those who needed me, but my immediate goal and focus was finishing the dissertation and defending it.

As the day of August 12th grew closer, the intensity of the situation swelled. Governor McAuliffe and I were good friends, and as he and I spoke about different things, he always sent his well wishes, along with his assurance that the city would have the resources we needed from a state police stand point. There was discussion between the mayor, myself, and other officials/high level staff about bringing in the National Guard. Those ideas were soon placed aside as a clearer plan came to fruition. We were close to a week away from the event, and our City Manager and Police Chief decided that due to potential security and safety issues, it would best to officially grant the permit to Jason Kessler, but to not allow him to have his event at Emancipation Park, but instead at a larger venue, McIntire Park. Here is the official report from the local newspaper, The Daily Progress:

126

Citing concerns for security and safety, Charlottesville officials on Monday said they will approve a demonstration permit for Saturday's Unite the Right rally organized by pro-white activists if the rally is moved to McIntire Park. But Jason Kessler, who is organizing the rally, says he won't accept the condition because McIntire Park lacks the symbolism provided by the statue of Confederate Gen. Robert E. Lee that has stood in Emancipation Park, recently renamed from Lee Park, since the 1920s. "The whole thing is in support of the Lee monument," Kessler said after the city's news conference announcing the decision to change the location.

"The fact that they'd try and move it away from the statue is, in itself, a violation of our free speech rights."

Kessler said he would seek legal recourse rather than move the rally. At the news conference, City Manager Maurice Jones said the size and nature of the demonstration for which Kessler submitted a permit application on May 30 has changed as more protesters and counter-protesters signed on. "Based on information provided to me by law enforcement officials, the city has decided to approve Mr. Kessler's application for a permit to hold a demonstration on the day and at the times requested, provided that he use McIntire Park, rather than Emancipation Park, for the demonstration," Jones said, reading from a prepared statement. "There is no doubt that Mr. Kessler has a First Amendment right to hold a demonstration and to express his views. Nor is there any doubt that we, as a city, have an obligation to protect those rights, the people who seek to exercise them, and the broader community in which they do," Jones said. "We have determined that we cannot do all of these things effectively if the demonstration is held in Emancipation Park."

Jones and other city officials declined to answer any questions during or after the news conference. The rally in Emancipation Park promised multiple planned protests and possibly thousands of protesters vehemently opposed to each other all crammed into a four-block area of downtown. That had city officials worried about public safety. The Unite the Right rally, scheduled for noon to 5 p.m. Saturday, is expected to be attended by members of the National Socialist Movement, the pro-secessionist League of the South and hundreds of their allies in the Nationalist Front and "alt-right" movement. According to permits acquired from the city by University of Virginia professor Walt Heinecke, counter-protesters are expected to gather at the park and at nearby McGuffey Park and Justice Park, recently renamed from Jackson Park. The alt-right groups indicated they would try to bring as many as 1,000 protesters to the park, and local chapters of Showing Up for Racial Justice and Black Lives Matter also have posted calls on social media for people to join them in counter-protest.

Congregate Charlottesville, a multi-denominational clergy group, made a July call for 1,000 clergy, especially white clergy, to attend the rally in protest. Officials on Monday declined to estimate the number of protesters they expect, but estimates bandied about by local businesses and organizers range from 2,000 to 8,000. Police said the anticipated number of protesters would make it difficult to ensure public safety if the Unite the Right rally were held at Emancipation Park. "Having the demonstration at McIntire Park is safer because the park is large enough to accommodate the size of the anticipated crowd," said Charlottesville Police Chief Al Thomas. "It also avoids a situation whereby overflow crowds spill into the streets, as would likely occur at Emancipation Park."

Thomas, who also read from a prepared statement, said the larger park will allow more security, better emergency medical care and other services. "Law enforcement also will have the room needed to maneuver and direct crowds toward safety in case of a disturbance," he said. "Additionally, we can more effectively stage other public safety resources that would allow for immediate response, if needed." Social activists said they question the safety of relocating to McIntire Park because it has limited entrances and exits should something happen. One referred to the park on Twitter as a potential "battlefield."

"McIntire Park has limited ingress and egress points and has natural choke points," said Emily Gorcenski, a

Charlottesville social activist who questioned whether the relocation would provide more safety. "If you're out in the heat at McIntire, forget it. There is no shade."

Saturday's events come in the wake of a July 8th Ku Klux Klan rally that brought about 50 Klan members and 1,000 counter-protesters to Jackson Park. That rally was loud, but nonviolent until the Klan members left after about 45 minutes. Protesters derided both Klan members and police as the Klan exited. Video taken at the protests shows some protesters hurling bottles and objects at police. Police declared an unlawful assembly and shot three tear gas canisters to break up the crowd. By the end, 23 people had been arrested. Police and protesters disagreed about whether the tear gas was necessary, with police saying that at least one officer was doused with a protester's pepper spray and the protesters denying that it happened. Thomas said police support the right to demonstrate, but said the demonstrations need to be peaceful.

"I would remind everyone who plans to participate in these demonstrations or counter-demonstrations that you have a right to do so peacefully," Thomas said. Thomas also noted that the approaching rally has many in town worried for their safety. Citing that possibility, UVA President Teresa A. Sullivan last week advised staff, students and faculty to avoid the rally. "There is a credible risk of violence at this event, and your safety is my foremost concern," she wrote. The potential conflict has caused concern among businesses, especially on the

Downtown Mall. Business owners say they have discussed with police whether to be open as usual that day. Some have decided to close. Brazos Tacos and the McGuffey Art Center previously announced they would be closed Saturday. The Virginia Discovery Museum announced Monday that it will be closed Saturday. In a statement, the museum said the road closures expected downtown will make it too difficult for people to visit the children's museum.

"VDM is a resource for all children of our community, as we understand that children learn best in an inclusive environment," the statement read. "We seek to meet the interests, needs and abilities of all the children we serve and to create an environment in which differences are celebrated." Susan Payne, a spokeswoman for the Downtown Business Association of Charlottesville, on Monday said the association supports the city's move.

"This decision protects the safety of the community, as well as downtown properties, due to the anticipated increase in the size of the crowd," Payne said in a statement. "The size of the McIntire Park location provides more adequate parking and space for individuals attending the rally." Thomas asked that protesters from both camps to pledge to remain nonviolent. "I urge groups on both sides to publicly commit to a nonviolent assembly," he said. "Your commitment may influence the small minority that may seek to jeopardize public safety and will also serve to strengthen bonds throughout our community, reduce a growing cloud of fear, and emotionally disarm those who would delight in provoking others towards violent actions." Mayor Mike Signer said the City Council backs the decision to move the rally while supporting the right of opposing sides to demonstrate.

"Democracy can be noisy, and it can be messy," he said. "But by ensuring we protect both public safety and the Constitution through the city manager's decision, I firmly believe that we will emerge from the weekend of August 12th a stronger community than ever."

This decision was met with a great deal of pushback from a variety of people. Kessler was adamant that the rally had to be held in Emancipation Park, because that was where the Lee Statue was located.

Again, this was weird to me, because many of the people who he had coming to the event didn't even know about the statue. They were there to mainly stand up for the perseverance of a society that was purely white. Kessler was simply attempting to use the statue as the rallying call, but we all knew it was about more than that. With a new plan in place to move the rally to McIntire Park, also a well-known white racist from Charlottesville, we then had to begin looking at alternative options. Security and communication plans were made and sent out to patrol McIntire by law enforcement. Community groups and visitors were then making arrangements to hold counter protests there, as well as in other parts of the city. I got a call about putting together a sunrise service on August 12th at First Baptist Church on W. Main St., my home church, as well as the oldest African American church in the city. There was also plans for the clergy collective to host a community wide service at St. Paul's across the street from the University of Virginia on the evening of August 11th.

It was clear that the Clergy community and local activists were committed to standing up and doing what they could to rally the community together to be safe, to feel secure, and to be as prepared for the unknown as feasibly possible.

Chapter 14

Unlikely Foes

August 8, 2017 - Charlottesville, Virginia

While the large majority of the community was desperately asking for the city to do something to stop the rally, and to not allow for White Supremacists and Neo-Nazis who threatened violence to come to our city, we received a letter from the American Civil Liberaties Union (ACLU) and Rutherford Institute at the University of Virginia essentially vowing to protect the rights to free speech by Jason Kessler. The email read as follows: "Dear members of the Charlottesville City Council and City Manager Jones:

Attached please find a letter from The Rutherford Institute and the ACLU of Virginia regarding the revocation of the permit of "Unite the Right" to hold a demonstration in Emancipation Park on August 12, 2017.

135

As organizations committed to protecting constitutional and civil rights, we demand that the City withdraw its letter to Jason Kessler of August 7, 2017, revoking and otherwise rescinding the permit for that demonstration and provide assurances that the City will allow the "Unite the Right" demonstration as previously planned and approved by operation of law. We will need a response to this letter by noon (12:00 p.m.) August 9, 2017."

August 8, 2017 Mike Signer, Mayor (via e-mail msigner@charlottesville.org) Wes Bellamy, Vice-Mayor (via e-mail wbellamy@charlottesville.org) Kristin Szakos, Charlottesville City Council (via e-mail k.szakos@embarqmail.com) Kathy Galvin, Charlottesville City Council (via e-mail kgalvin@charlottesville.org) Bob Fenwick, Charlottesville City Council (via e-mail bfenwick@charlottesville.org) Maurice Jones, Charlottesville City Manager (vial e-mail mjones@charlottesville.org) –

Dear City Councilors and Mr. Jones, The City of Charlottesville's belated demand that the "Unite the Right" demonstration scheduled for August 12 move from its planned and approved location in Emancipation Park raises serious First Amendment concerns.

1. Opposition can be no basis for government action that would suppress the First Amendment rights of demonstrators, no matter how distasteful those views may be Both the timing and justification for the demand that organizers accept a move to McIntire Park show a

136

callous disrespect for the rights of free speech and assembly, forcing an 11th-hour relocation of the rally from the place chosen specifically because of its importance to the message of the rally organizers. While the message of the "Unite the Right" rally may raise strong feelings of opposition among area residents and political leaders, that opposition can be no basis for government action that would suppress the First Amendment rights of demonstrators who have acted according to the law.

2. Last-minute relocation undermines ability of demonstrators to effectively communicate their message The last-minute relocation by the City appears to be an attempt to undermine the ability of demonstrators to effectively communicate their message. Although event organizers submitted their application for the rally in Emancipation Park two months ago, the City is only now asserting that the event cannot be safely conducted in the park, a place chosen specifically by event organizers because of the symbolic significance of the Lee statute. This belated action by the City seriously undermines the ability of organizers to protect their legal rights to enforce their permit Mike Signer, Mayor, et al. August 8, 2017 Page 2 to rally in the park, a permit that was plainly approved under section 3.4.6 of the City's Special Events Regulations.

3. City must provide factual evidence to support its attendance estimate and justify revoking the permit to demonstrate in Emancipation Park It is also questionable

137

whether the City's demand, which is effectively a revocation of the permit to demonstrate in Emancipation Park, is justified by any provision of the Special Events Regulation. Revocation could only be justified under section 3.4.7 of the regulation on the basis that the event "presents a danger to public safety" or "cannot reasonably be accommodated in the particular area applied for[.]"

While the City relies upon a forecast that "many thousands" will attend the event, it has not disclosed the sources of the information it is relying on for that estimate and whether such sources have any factual basis. When First Amendment rights are at stake, the City should be transparent about the evidence and information underlying its action so that citizens can be sure that fears of overcrowding are not simply a pretext for censorship and meet the requirement for proof that a compelling government interest underlies its decision.

Moreover, demonstration organizers should be allowed to know the basis for the City's crowd projections so that they can defend the rights granted by the permit by challenging and rebutting the City's unilateral conclusion that the event poses a danger to public safety. The City's justification for revocation appears more specious in light of the City's approval of permits for opposing demonstrations on August 12th in Justice and McGuffey Parks which will reportedly expect attendance of greater than 1000 persons. Furthermore, "Unite the Right" organizers reportedly offered to allow City officials to limit access to Emancipation Park during their event to prevent overcrowding. Thus, fears of overcrowding that would lead to public safety concerns appear to be a pretext for silencing the "Unite the Right" demonstration. 4. If the City is justifying its relocation of the rally elsewhere based on the presence of counterdemonstrators, that constitutes an unconstitutional "hecklers' veto." To the extent the City is relying on the presence of counterdemonstrators for its revocation of the Emancipation Park permit, it is violating the fundamental principle that the rights of speech and assembly may not be restricted because demonstrators may be met by opposition. There is no place for a "hecklers' veto" under the First Amendment.

4. Any decision that the demonstration under the permit poses a threat to public safety should be based solely on the plans and actions of the "Unite the Right" organizers, not of those who plan to be present in opposition. Otherwise, 1 That section provides "[a]ll requests for demonstration permits shall be DEEMED GRANTED, subject to all applicable limitations and restrictions, unless denied within ten business days following the application for a permit[.]" City of Charlottesville Standard Operating Procedure Policy No. 100-04. 2 Id. 3 National Socialist White People's Party v. Ringers, 473 F.2d 1010, 1014 n.4 (4th Cir. 1973).

See also, Christian Knights of KKK v. District of Columbia, 972 F.2d 365 (D.C. Cir 1992). 4 Christian Knights of Ku Klux Klan Invisible Empire, Inc. v. Stuart, 934 F.2d 318

(4th Cir. 1991). Mike Signer, Mayor, et al. August 8, 2017 Page 3 hecklers and counter-demonstrators could always shut down speech they disagree with by manufacturing threats to public safety.

5. The City must act in accordance with the law, no matter how distasteful that may be to members of the community The City must act in accordance with the law, even if doing so is distasteful to members of the community who disagree with the views espoused by the "Unite the Right" organizers. At the very least, the City must explain in more than just generalities its reasons for concluding that the demonstration cannot safely be held in Emancipation Park. It must allow the organizers the opportunity to dispel fears or concerns about the rally. Otherwise, it appears that the City's revocation of the permit is based only upon public opposition to the message of the demonstration, which would constitute a violation of the organizers' fundamental First Amendment rights. As organizations committed to protecting constitutional and civil rights, we demand that the City withdraw its letter to Jason Kessler of August 7, 2017, revoking and otherwise rescinding the permit for a demonstration in Emancipation Park on August 12, 2017, and provide assurances that the City will allow the "Unite the Right" demonstration as previously planned and approved by operation of law. We will need a response to this letter by noon (12:00 p.m.) August 9, 2017.

Sincerely, Claire Guthrie Gastanaga, Executive Director John W. Whitehead, President ACLU Foundation of

Virginia The Rutherford Institute claire@acluva.org
johnw@rutherford.org

To say that I was absolutely, utterly flabbergasted and dumbfounded would be a complete understatement...

The same group, the ACLU, that I had went out on a limb for at a city council meeting to agree with their demands for accountability and responsibility in regards to the actions of the police on July 8th, came forward and defended a White Supremacists less than a month later.

I had my own personal thoughts and feelings about the Rutherford Institute, but I will admit that I was still shocked that they would go to this measure. Furthermore, demanding that our city attorney, who was literally working around the clock as it was, respond to their letter by the next day was also very disrespectful. This was one instance where I thought that White Supremacy works in a variety of ways. I couldn't help but ponder if a group of Black Men had planned a similar demonstration, would they receive the same level of support? The Unite the Right Rally had "Civil Rights" groups fighting for them, donors from around the country donating funds to sponsor people from across the country to come and participate in the rally, militias who vowed to come and protect them, and people making documentaries and videos in support of their actions. So, when people would say that this is my fault, or I started all of this, I could only laugh.

141

This was systemic.

Miraculously, our city attorney got a response to the ACLU and Rutherford Institute the next day, August 9th, only to be told that they were disappointed with our response and that they have taken on Kessler as a client to defend his first amendment rights. The initial shock had wore off as far as I was concerned, and at that point, I was learning to expect the unexpected.

After being briefed, it became apparent that the ACLU and Kessler were going to push for an emergency injunction to allow the Unite the Right to have their rally at Emancipation Park. While I was hoping that the Federal Judge would understand not only the potential threat of violence, but also the pure precedence that was being set, it was becoming more and more clear to me that the city, the community as a whole, the state, and the nation still didn't quite get it. Some people did, but a large majority of others did not. It was going to take something tragic to happen to get people's attention. People from the community crying out and pleading for something to change was not enough to make our legal system understand, as the laws were not created to protect the oppressed, only the oppressor.

My friends, family, and what seemed like a ton of people who I normally didn't interact with, were all calling, texting, and hitting me up on social media. There was one consistent theme in all of their messages and conversations, "We know how you can get, you need to be safe." I was reassuring everyone that I was fine, and more than anything else, that I was prepared for whatever was going to happen, to happen. A few guys from the barbershop told me that they wanted to meet later that night, and it was mandatory. I'm normally not one who likes being told what to do, but I sensed the seriousness of the tone in their voices, and I told them that I would be there after I finished practicing my dissertation in Petersburg (Yes, that was still scheduled for August 11th at 1:00 PM). I walked in, sat down, and knew immediately that this was not going to go well.

These guys, most of whom were from here, who had been here for years and had a strong footprint in the city, were there that night for one reason: to tell me that I wasn't going to the rally on Saturday.

We had a long conversation, and we went back and forth about why I felt I needed to be there, how I didn't want to let the community down. I refused to allow this group to come to our city and simply think that they can takeover without any kind of pushback. For them, my brothers standing before me in the barber shop - it was more so about safety. They were there for the KKK rally and believed had I been at that one that things would not have turned out well for me. In their eyes, going to this rally would be even worse.

I was hellbent on going to Unite the Right, and eventually they realized that the only way to stop me was by them physically knocking me out. We agreed on a compromise.

143

I was scheduled to say a few words at the sunrise service on Saturday morning, and I was going to be in the march from the church to the Jefferson School African American Heritage Center. It was decided that they would be with me at all times, they would personally be responsible for all of my whereabouts, and I was to leave immediately after I was finished. My wife was another one who was on equally on edge. She too was worried that something bad was going to happen, and wanted me to come down south with her and the rest of my family. I just couldn't quite go through with leaving. I told her that I would, but deep down inside, I thought it was the coward's way out.

Mind over matter, and being safe was the plan...
but plans were made to be broken right?

Chapter 15

The Weekend of Hate... and Triumph:

This is Charlottesville

On August 11th, the beginning of the worst case scenario began. If there was ever a cloud over our city before, the Friday morning of August 11th felt like the darkness before a thunderstorm. Many of the White Nationalists, White Supremacists, Neo-Nazi's, Neo-Confederates, and other groups that pushed a pro-white and conservative agenda were in the city. People who lived within the city and the entire surrounding area as a whole were all on edge. Some people had reported seeing them walking around the city. There were other reports and social media messages of a few scuffles, but nothing would be close to what we were about to experience.

I jogged over to Emancipation Park and the statue of Robert E. Lee that morning like I normally did. This time was different though. The police were setting up barricades to separate protestors and counter protestors, and a lot of people were walking around –

nervously. It was only 8:00 AM, and the feeling of anticipation and tension was already in the air.

A homeless man, who had always been cordial with me stopped me and said, "I wish you could stop this. Nothing about this weekend is going to be good..." I agreed with him, tried to smile and reassure him that things were going to be ok, but I couldn't. We didn't quite know what was going to happen, and that was the most frightening part of it all. Would we be like Berkeley, would we be like Portland, or even worse, would Charlottesville become a hashtag, we just didn't know.

My colleagues on council were all talking about going to different events throughout the weekend, and as they asked me if I was going to be at the protest, I told them that I would, but I wouldn't be at the entire thing. They all said they believed that to be a "smart call." I didn't, but I didn't want to argue. I knew where my heart was. It was with the people. I left for Petersburg and Virginia State University around 10:00 AM, met with my dissertation Chair, and defended my dissertation:

"Perceptions of Central Virginia Educators and Community Stakeholders towards the Competency of African American Male Educators for Grades K–12."

My wife, friends, and many family members attended. Things went well and I officially became: Dr. Wes Bellamy. It was ok... a moment that I had worked much of my professional career for was just... okay.

148

I understood why:
My mind was in Charlottesville.

I had just completed one of the biggest accomplishments of my life, entered into a fraternity of scholars that less than one percent of the U.S. population belonged to, but all I that I could really think about was getting back to Charlottesville and preparing for what was about to come next. My wife and I went to Applebees after, and she said to me over our meal:

"For someone who just did what a lot of people dream of doing, you sure seem somber." All I could say to her in response was, *"it's hard to explain"*. The unknown was before us, and I was struggling with the thoughts of what everyone else was saying. Was this really all my fault? Did the White supremacists really come here because of me? Should I have just left the statue alone? Should I have quit city council a while back and just found a job elsewhere? Am I going to die this weekend? How am I going to be safe? Will this be the last time that I see my wife? Were the guys from the barbershop right?

As I kissed my wife goodbye that evening as she departed with our children to go up to South Carolina and I headed back to Charlottesville, something told me that this was going to be a weekend that we would never forget.

I was informed by the police that it wouldn't be a good idea to stay at my house, so I made other arrangements. I went back to Emancipation Park as it was now roughly 5:30 PM. People were there, and I ran into a couple who was visiting from Colorado, and were crying. They were filled with despair and hopelessness about what may potentially happen this weekend. A few young people were also in the park, saw us chatting and came up to me and asked to take a picture. I told them all that everything was going to be okay, and that we had to remain positive. I was lying to them. I didn't know what was going to happen, but I knew that if I looked sad, so would they. They needed something to believe in. At that moment, I told myself that things *were* going to be okay.

We were made for times like these.

I went back to where I was staying, changed clothes, and headed to the Church service at St. Pauls. I told myself that positive energy would be the only thing that I focus on this weekend. No matter what happens, I would remain positive. I would lead. I would put my faith in God, and trust that everything would work out as it should be... I would soon be tested.

One of my best friends, Will Jones, met me at the Church as his wife was singing in the choir. The venue was packed to the brim, and when I got there, they told me I had to enter in the back, because they were at capacity. Luckily, they saved me a seat in the front, and the energy in the room was electric to say the least. Preachers,

150

Clergy Members, and Evangelists from all over the country were in attendance. Community Members from all over the city and state were there. Songs were sang and the word was preached for every ear in the room. Our spirits were more than lifted.

The preacher that evening – a fierce sister by the name of Rev. Traci Blackmon gave a powerful sermon about cutting off the head of White Supremacy. She discussed how we can't run from it, we can't hide from it, but instead we have to stand up to it and deal with it. It was one of the most powerful things that I had ever heard. What we soon found out was that while we were hearing about cutting off the heads of White Supremacy and fighting for what was right, the ugly faces of hate were outside and surrounding the 500+ people inside the Church. I'm not sure what the infatuation is with these guys and tiki torches, but they seem to be really fond of them. An announcement was made as the service was coming to an end, that a couple hundred White Supremacists were outside of the church and it was best for everyone to stay inside.

As all of this was occurring, my phone was also going off with all kinds of messages and alerts regarding Kessler. The Federal Judge in the case pertaining to whether or not the city had to allow Kessler to be able to have his rally at Emancipation Park, decided to grant an injunction to the ACLU and Kessler which cleared the way for him to be able to have his rally at Emancipation Park with the Lee statue and not, McIntire Park.

151

This had been the decision that I was afraid of – delivered at the absolute worst time as I sat surrounded by terrified faces. I continued reading for clarity:

In essence, Kessler's attorney, Victor Glasberg, argued that the city changed the permit location for Kessler's rally because city officials did not like Kessler's message. As evidence for that, Glasberg pointed to a few tweets from Charlottesville Mayor Mike Signer that criticized the alt-right and encouraged people to stand against it. But Charlottesville City Attorney Craig Brown said the city manager, Maurice Jones, made the decision to move the rally, not Signer. Brown also argued that the city gave ample reason to move the rally for public safety reasons, and that the nature of Kessler's message had nothing to do with that decision. Glasberg also criticized the city for trying to move Kessler's permit, but not doing the same for other groups with permits to rally downtown on Saturday.

Brown said that the only other permit that was granted was to a group called Peoples Action for Racial Justice, or PARJ, and the city did not see the need to change that event's location because online posts showed that less than 100 people were signed up to attend the event.

In court, apparently there was also extensive discussion about whether the rally would actually be safer if done in McIntire Park instead of Emancipation Park. Brown argued that McIntire Park is safer because there is more space and it would be easier to keep Kessler's supporters separate from counter-protest groups.

152

Both sides conceded that there were expected to be more counter-protesters at the rally than Kessler supporters. Attorneys representing downtown businesses also testified that they were concerned about property damage if the rally is allowed to stay in Emancipation Park.

I closed my phone. Very few people in the church were aware of the judge's decision. The immediate issue however was not what would happen the next day, it was the present sense of danger that was happening right then, that most feared. A sense of panic rushed over the church as it was repeated that everyone needed to stay in their chairs and not be dismissed for safety reasons. However, the leaders did a great job of getting the choir to sing more songs and of reassuring everyone that they were safe. "This is only a precaution." They affirmed the crowd and let them know that staying inside for a short amount of time was best. Simultaneously, beyond the church, Kessler and his crew were parading around the University and fell upon the statue of Thomas Jefferson where a group of students and community members had surrounded the statue – holding Black Lives Matter propaganda: posters, banners. Kessler and his followers begun singing white supremacy songs and chants as they closed in around them as an intimidation tactic.

To say that they were some of the boldest people in the city at that moment and time was an understatement. I began calling up CPD members and unfortunately was being told that there was nothing that they could do at the moment, because the event was taking place on

Grounds (that's what UVA calls their campus) and not in their jurisdiction. What I later came to find out was that just as the local activists had warned, the group of White Supremacists had planned an initial rally on the 11th with tiki torches to take back the university.

According to people that I spoke with on the CPD, communication was made between CPD and the UVA police that this rally was going to take place that night. It was asked whether or not UVA police wanted the CPD to be there as back up or to assist with what was going on, and they were told no. UVA PD was supposed to be on top of the situation and handling it, but that's not what occurred. Not only were the people inside the church protected mainly by brave community members and activists, the young people and community members who had stood up to the White Supremacists in front of the Jefferson Statue were fighting alone for a while.

There was little to no police presence to assist them.

It took a while for the CPD to eventually say that they were going to intervene no matter what, and declared an unlawful assembly and encouraged everyone to leave. This was after a few fights, more scuffles, and clear intimidation by hundreds of White Supremacists with burning torches chanting "White Lives Matter" "You Will Not Replace Us" and "Jews Will Not Replace Us."

While the rally and counter protest was eventually broken up, the people from the church were also eventually escorted to their cars, and things calmed down... But the tone had been set. The Unite the Right was here. They were going to do whatever they needed to in order to provoke people to fight, and they wanted violence.

In my mind, we now had two clear issues. As I was escorted to my car, I looked across the street and caught a scene reminiscent of the one in May. Hundreds of white people with lighted torches standing beside a statue. As I attempted to walk over, I was stopped by friends and told that I had to go home. The moment the detractors saw me, they would look to do something stupid in an attempt to try and make a name for themselves. It was a tough pill to swallow, but something that had to be done. As the police broke up the event, it was clear. If this is what happened on day one, then tomorrow was going to be even worse. It was also tough to process and understand why the Federal judge would allow for the rally to be held in Emancipation Park the next day. I know he had seen the threats, the mere size of the park, and the potential for a combustible situation. It appeared that all of it was headed for a disaster.

However, those were only things that I thought in my mind. In my outwardly appearance, I smiled, looked on with confidence as if things were going to be ok, and promised the people who were asking me what to do next, that we had everything under control. I returned to

155

the place where I was staying, called my wife and let her know that I was safe, prayed and asked God for strength and guidance, and finally... went to sleep. I had to be up by 4:30 AM to be back at the church by 5:30 AM for the morning service. Dr. Cornell West had informed me that I shouldn't be late, so I figured I should listen.

Admittedly so, I didn't sleep most of the night. My mind wouldn't stop racing... So, I spent most of it praying instead. I didn't know what was going to happen, but I knew that in my mind, it was going to be a battle.

I drove to First Baptist in silence. No Jeezy, No Chance the Rapper, No R&B, no nothing. Just silence. The sun had yet to come out. Few cars were on the road. It was a surreal moment. I knew that after today, things would never be the same. My sister Shemica and brother Leon were both coming down from Richmond for the rally. My brothers who were there to protect me, met me at the church.

Upon arrival, I embraced my brother Deacon Don Gathers, and his energy was one of a warrior prepared for battle. I embraced and hugged Dr. Cornell West, and in his loving way he made a joke about the day. We sat in the Pastor's office and prayed. He told me that he had been in this position before and that things would be just as God wanted them to be. I too believed the same thing. We were here at this moment, at this time, for a specific reason. The service was packed, and I only remember saying a few words about how we must not allow for evil

156

to win. We could not allow for those who were determined to break us apart accomplish their goal.

Dr. West spoke in great detail about the power of doing what was right, right now. How he could love the person and hate the sin that is in a person. How we must also be willing to do whatever it took for us to win. This was a marathon and not a sprint. We then gave everyone instructions to meet us outside on the church steps. Something was off. I had requested a police escort for the entire group of nearly 500 people who were marching from the Church to the Jefferson School African American Heritage Center, and from the Center to McGuffey Park which was adjacent to Emancipation Park. However, strangely enough, none of those law enforcement officers showed up.

While still inside the church, a short announcement was made that those who had emergency training and were prepared to walk with Dr. West and the Clergy members to conjure in the back of the church. I had the training that they spoke of, yet Dr. West told me explicitly that I couldn't go with him on this pilgrimage. He told me to walk with my people because they needed me. Where he was going, he wasn't sure if he would be coming back. It was both a sobering moment, but also an enlightening one. As aforementioned, we all have a role to play in this. He was not in Charlottesville to be the face of the movement. He was there to speak the word of God, but to also directly confront the Hate that was ahead of us. I could not go with him because that wasn't what I was made or destined to do. My job and role at that point was to inform everyone outside that we were stronger together and march with the people to the Heritage Center. And that's exactly what I did.

We paraded in the middle of W. Main St. loudly proclaiming that this little light of ours was going to shine! Upon arrival at the Jefferson School Heritage Center, I saw my sister, Dr. Andrea Douglas, and a larger group of an additional 200-300 people. This felt great. Not because there was a lot of us, but because our community accepted the challenge to stand up and speak out. It now felt like we had the energy and momentum. We were prepared to stand tall for our community. We would not let hate win.

Brother Dr. Walter Heinicke had reserved the McGuffey Park right across the way from Emancipation Park and had arranged for his rally to begin hours before the Unite the Right Rally was scheduled to start. We arrived at the park around 9am. The Clergy collective had members and people from literally all over the country there. We had people standing proud. Standing tall. Prepared to defend our city. After saying a few words and leading a few chants, my team quickly reminded me that I was not allowed to stay at the rally for long. It was roughly 10:30am, and we had witnessed several White Supremacists walk by, stare at us, point at me, and then move along. It was a scene reminiscent of a movie. People literally walking down the street with machine guns, shields and swords, and all kinds of weapons.

I was approached by a couple of state police officers and told that they too had instructions to walk me out of the park and to the vehicles that were waiting for me. I reluctantly obliged and walked from the park, through the downtown mall, and up to W. Main St. I stopped and took a look around while I was crossing the Downtown Mall. It was the first time that I had ever felt a spirit of true despair in our city. It was a ghost town, until I saw out of the corner of my eye Dr. West and others walking in a small crew at an expeditious pace. It would later be found out that they were walking straight to the Park to confront the members of the Unite the Right, in an attempt to pray and deny them entry into the park.

After I was escorted out of the park, I called my wife and let her know that I was safe and that everything was ok. I then did something that I hadn't anticipated, but I believed to be necessary. I told her that I love her more than anything, but I couldn't leave the state today. I had to be in Charlottesville with my people. I promised her that I would be safe, to keep my head, and to be here when she returned. She didn't put up a fight, as I believe she understood and knew the immediate need that I felt to be in the city. My brothers, my protectors, and those who were there to simply keep me safe did not know that I was staying. I told them that I was getting on the road with my friends from Richmond, and then heading south. In actuality, we simply went and got some food, and then I returned. I let them know when I got back, dealt with the backlash, and then proceeded to be with the people.

159

It was now close to 11:30 or Noon and a state of Emergency had been declared by Governor McAuliffe. I got a phone call from a friend in the Governor's office asking about my whereabouts and of what was happening? After a brief discussion leading to them informing me that they were coming down to Charlottesville – I decided to check the scene outside.

As I peered out my window and looked around the city and onto downtown Charlottesville for that matter, I didn't know if I was in Charlottesville or a third world country the way people were fighting, pointing guns, and running around the streets to wreck havoc. I was extremely shocked to see the police watching the fights and not doing anything to stop it. A few officers literally watched people in full blown fist fights and stood idle.

Communications were flying back and forth between city staff and council, but on the actual street, our worst fears were materializing. As people paraded around the street with weapons clearly trying to scare people or push them to do something that would allow them to retaliate with violence, I immediately thought back to moments in time in which good vs. evil was fought – specifically revolving around race. One of the biggest differences from then and now and one that was both eye opening in different ways was the fact that most of the people who were fighting were white. Obviously, all of the people who were there for the actual Unite the Right rally were white, but a large majority of those who were fighting back against them were also white. In the weeks leading up to UTR, there was an awakening of sorts that was taking place throughout the community. In the community meetings, in the city council meetings, on the street, and on social media, I was seeing more and more white people say things like "this was their opportunity to stand up for what was right." They believed that they had an obligation as white people to use their privilege for good, to use their voices for good, and if need be, put their bodies on the line to fight back against hate.

I was hearing more and more from people who didn't look like me. They were adamant that because much of the hate that was coming towards people of color was coming from white people and since the systems and laws in place were created by white people, that other whites had to do what they could to try and right the wrongs of the past. I couldn't say that I disagreed with them, but I did think that it was an interesting position to take. It was appreciated, it was truly something that was necessary, but nonetheless, it was different.

A large majority of the black people that I spoke with were clear that they weren't going downtown that day. Several encouraged me to not attend. Many people of color believed that it wasn't our fight and that the White Supremacists' minds were not going to be changed by black people confronting them. That instead, they would be more prone to listen to other white people, and as a person of color, their time would be better served protecting their own communities, their own peace of mind, and their own bodies.

With this in mind, I would say that less than 20% of the people who were counter protesting were black.

I decided to take to the streets to get a better vantage point. While out, I saw some of my students, who were, understandably so, emotional wrecks. It's tough for someone to be so young and to witness such hate. Some of my male students were really upset that this kind of rally was allowed to happen in our city. Some of them said they heard the people there looking for me and were concerned about my safety. I told them to not worry about me, and to be safe, but in all honesty, I would be lying if I didn't say that I was a little worried. Things were literally spiraling out of control all around me. The police were trying to force people to leave, and it was at that time, that my sister Shemica told me that I should record something on social media and encourage people to get to a safe space. I did as she said.

After recording the video – ironically, while the White Supremacists were fighting for what they believed in – a group of young African American entrepreneurs were less than a mile away at Tonsler Park preparing to give away over 200 book bags, school supplies, and food in an effort to get young people in need ready to go back to school. I couldn't walk away from an opportunity to help them give back. I then received a phone call from a young woman who had risen in the community as a strong community leader, advocate, and activist – Nikuyah Walker.

162

She asked me profusely did I see what happened 4th Street. I hadn't... moments later my phone began to blow up with text messages from people all over the city asking me was I safe. I wasn't aware in that moment of what was going on but I knew I had to find out. I told the young entrepreneurs running the Back To School Bash that I would be back – I wasn't sure how true that was, but I knew I had to make my way back to the center of the chaos. Before I could get to far, I then got a call from the Governor's office asking where I was at the exact moment. This let me know that things were really bad. After a brief conversation, , I was told to get to the Downtown Mall as soon as possible. When I got there, I couldn't even properly walk over because the scene was absolutely chaotic.

People were running every way imaginable, crying uncontrollably, as fire trucks, ambulances, and police sirens blazed in the background. Still not sure what had happened, I was grabbed by a police officer and told "Councilor Bellamy, I need to get you to safety, immediately." I was rushed to a remote area in which I was then told grimly that several people were struck by a vehicle. A brief update was provided by our City Manager, Maurice Jones, and my heart absolutely broke.

I stood, numb, as a variety of people began explaining to me what they had saw. Bodies literally flying in the air on impact and a car that ran everyone over who had fallen to the ground, reversed, and then ran everyone over again. I couldn't swallow. I couldn't breathe and even

163

more so, I couldn't believe what I was hearing. Charlottesville had turned into a monster of a place in a matter of hours in which White Supremacists attacked everyday people like wild animals attack their prey, and now we had serious injuries on our hands.

I must admit, at that moment, I was out of answers. The faux confidence I had trained myself to wear shattered at my feet. I thought about the events of the night before and being surrounded in a church in which people were vulnerable and open to attack by these same White Supremacists. I thought about the images of the morning and throughout the day of seeing armed White people with guns, shields... looking to create chaos. Now, here we were... people being run over by vehicles, beaten with all kinds of objects, with a muddled sense of lawlessness purveying throughout the city.

My heart sank.

Damn, is this my fault? Should I have just left the whole damn thing alone? *Is this my fault*? I sulked in that for a minute or two before my phone starting ringing again.

"Wes, where you at? I thought that you were running home to bring the extra school supplies that you had at your house?"

Chapter 16

A Bright Light On A Dark Day

While White Supremacists and Neo Nazi's were wreaking havoc on our city, less than two miles away from the Downtown Mall was something incredible going on at Tonsler Park. I had mentioned that I saw them briefly but that doesn't give them or that moment any justice. These few, outstanding young brothers and sisters from Charlottesville and the surrounding areas, had made an effort to not allow for August 12th to be a bad day for the city. They coordinated gathering nearly 150 book bags - I had a few left over from my annual back to school bash and wanted to support their cause. After hearing what I heard Downtown I was glad to have received the call to remind me to go back home and rush back over to the park. We filled all of the bookbags up with school supplies as a DJ pulled up and the music started blasting. Food was coming off the grill, and the mood was festive, yet serious. Many of the people who were at the cookout weren't aware of what was going on downtown. You see, for a lot of black people, this issue wasn't necessarily ours to fight. To me, it was a conflicting feeling, but one that truly represented Charlottesville. It's a complex city with complex issues, and not everyone feels like every fight is their own for a variety of reasons. And as I mentioned before, most of the people involved in the chaos that day were white.

My sister, Whitney pulled up and then pulled me into her car, and started to give me a talk. Her boyfriend, one of my good friends in the city, Big Will, the same guy who went around the city with me before the KKK rally in July telling people to not fall for the bait, was also in the car. Both said to me, I needed to be here, and not downtown. I needed to be with the people who had my back, and made sure that I was safe. Those people were at Tonsler Park. I looked around, and took in what they were saying.

At the top of the entrance to Tonsler Park were about 8-10 brothers who were also armed, and watching every car that drove by. They were set on ensuring that every person in the park would be safe. They were prepared to die if they had to for the safety of every single body that was inside the park. Councilor Kristin Szakos asked me where I was. Once I told her she then joined me at the park. She had been at the NAACP event that took place in Albemarle County, but her heart was heavy. We both looked at each other and then hugged each other. We knew that this was going to be a day that our city never forgot, and it was tough. We then parted ways, but not without exchanging a few encouraging words first. We promised to keep our spirits high. We vowed to not allow the detractors and supremacists to break our spirits. We couldn't. After she left, a little kid walked over to me and asked me "Who was that White Woman? Is she one of the bad people here to hurt us?" I looked down at him and smiled. I told him that she's on our side today, she's been on our side, and she's always on our side. I told him what I had learned over time in Charlottesville. "A person doesn't have to look like you, grow up like you, or even be like you to ride for you."

I smiled faintly as I thought about what was before me. We had 200 book bags and a full line wrapped around the park with kids, families, and parents all having a good time while getting their school supplies, kid games, and food. Brothers and sisters were laughing and smiling. Things looked as if it was a happy day. We knew there was a dark cloud just a few blocks away, but that didn't mean that there wasn't a community need that still needed to be filled. Domestic terrorists may have been in the city, but we still had babies and young people who needed school supplies and their spirits uplifted. There were still families that needed to know that someone had their back. These young black men, basically provided a sense of light in a really dark time.

https://education.good.is/articles/teacher-block-party-charlottesville-school-supplies

As the back to school drive was coming to an end, my mood began to shift. The day was hectic and all over the place, and now I was going from feeling proud that our community was able to still do something powerful in the midst of a tragedy, to learning more about what was

169

really at stake/play here. I got a call from the Governor's office that he was en-route to Charlottesville. Mayor Signer and I had a brief conversation, and it was decided that we would go to the County Office Building for a briefing about the current situation. There was an eerie feeling of darkness and a huge grey cloud over the city. No one really knew what was going to happen next.

As night fell, we all had so many unanswered questions. Were the White Supremacists' were gearing up for another attack that night? Were those innocent people who were ran over by that car still alive? And was it true that the White Supremacists had tried to go into one of our most predominate African-American neighborhoods - Friendship Court, and try and attack our residents?

We didn't know... The scene at the County Office Building was something reminiscent of a check point in a war zone. I was thinking to myself, is this really going on in Charlottesville? Before turning into the parking lot, my car was stopped, thoroughly searched, and I was also forced to show my city council credentials before being let in. As I walked into the building, a building that I literally went into once a week, it looked nothing like the local government facility that I was accustomed to. It was heavily secured with military and law enforcement personnel. It was also a reminder that this was a very serious situation. Governor McAulife, a man who I have the utmost respect for, and consider a friend and mentor walked in, and greeted everyone. We were all escorted

170

to a secluded and isolated part of the building due to the high amount of press that was in attendance.

At this point all five of the city councilors had arrived and the look of despair was on the face of everyone. I'm normally the one that tries to keep the mood light by cracking a joke or two or by saying something to bring about a smile, but there was nothing that I could say. Governor McAuliffe began to talk about what he had seen, what he had been briefed on, and then said something that I did not expect to hear. Apparently, there had been a helicopter crash, and both of the individuals flying the helicopter were his personal airmen. They both had passed away during the crash. We were looking at a situation in which we had deranged people literally come and invade our city, create havoc and terror and now there were casualties as a result.

There was a car that plowed into a group of people who were just walking in the street. We didn't know how many people were injured, or who they were, and now we have news that there was also a helicopter crash. This was a tough day, and it was only 6:30 PM. With the governor, our city manager, our police chief, and several of the top brass from the Virginia State Police, we had to make another tough decision. Would we implement a curfew in the city? We went into executive emergency closed session as a city council to authorize Chief Thomas with the authority to be able to implement a curfew. There was a great deal of back and forth about what we should do, but ultimately it was up to Chief

Thomas. The concern was twofold. One, we would have to be able to get a handle on the situation, and ensure that everyone was safe, but at the same time, we didn't want people to feel like they are prisoners in their own community. I had just left an event in which it was rather clear, the people who came to the community cookout and back pack giveaway did not really know or understand about all of the other things that were going on in the city. To a certain extent, they were simply living their lives as normal, and they wanted to continue to be able to do so. Should they be punished? It was a very delicate situation, that we ultimately left in the hands of the Chief. He had the authority to do so, and it was up to him if he chose to carry it out.

Simultaneously while this meeting/decision was taking place, we had to prepare to stand with our Governor and other elected officials, law enforcement officers, and people involved in the decision-making process for a press conference. It was clearly communicated that we rejected all of the attacks, the racist rhetoric, and the acts of intimidation. I'm not really sure how it happened, but I ended up standing right behind the Governor and the podium, and soon became a meme. While everyone began to speak and say their parts, Governor McAuliffe went into a speech that I will never forget. He spoke forcefully and with conviction about how we must stand united and we will not cower. He has always been a great speaker, and on this day, he sounded like a Baptist preacher on a Sunday morning before making the final alter call for salvation. I stood behind him shaking my head in approval and was proud of his words about patriotism, heroes, and truly being an American... that is until he mentioned something to the effect that real heroes and patriots were Thomas Jefferson, George Washington, and the like. I didn't want to be rude, but it was hard to control myself. I wanted to ask him what the hell was he doing? Don't get me wrong a lot of people have a lot of love for Thomas Jefferson, but to me, he was one hand a man that made strides for the area and for th country as a whole, but also on the other hand, a slave owner, rapist of Sally Hemmings, and a man who believed that people who looked like me were less than human and didn't even have the ability to emote.

Now, I'm not here to judge anyone, because clearly, it's well documented here how much I had to grow, but to laud Jefferson during that moment didn't sit well with me. Apparently, it was visual for the entire country, as I went from vehemently shaking my head in approval to an abrupt stop once Jefferson was mentioned.

It wasn't that I was disagreeing with the Governor on the basis of what he was saying, as I believe that he was right that the cowards who came to our city were not patriots, but I think it was another instance in which we all had to undergo in the process of "waking up." People from all over the country laud Thomas Jefferson for the work that he did for the country, but that does not negate the fact that he raped his slaves, Sally Hemmings to be specific, fathered children with his slaves, prohibited his slaves from being freed, and, as I said, went as far as to state

173

that he believed that Black people did not have the ability to emote. In my eyes, and in the eyes of black people across the country, that is not the person that needed to be referenced during the time in which White Supremacists had just ravished and terrorized our streets. Once the governor finished his speech, all of the councilors and everyone else parted ways. Nightfall was upon us. We, the city, was hoping for the best, but just like everything else that day, we had no idea what was about to happen.

I sat out to hit the neighborhoods and check on people from around the way. It was an eerie sight throughout the city. It had begun to rain – a visual and metaphoric washing away of the events of earlier played out in my mind. Televisions throughout homes showed the painful images of a vehicle plowing through a crowd. The nation was watching us, but inside the city, this was not a movie or some reality show. This was real life. A lot of people were staying inside of their homes, as no one really knew if the deranged people from earlier in the afternoon had left, or if they were still here, waiting for another attack once the darkness came.

As I went into one of our infamous public housing sites, Westhaven, I was approached by residents from throughout the neighborhood. They asked was I okay, and if they were going to be safe. The looks on their faces were somewhere between fear, and a savage willingness to do whatever they humanly had to in order to protect their neighborhood, their community, their family, their

174

city. I told them that the worst was behind us, but that was a lie. I smiled and tried to pretend that everything was ok, but that too was a lie. The truth was that I didn't know. I desperately wanted to believe that everything was ok, but I really didn't know. The police told us that we would be safe, but that appeared to be a lie. The community was in a whirlwind.

Now, I found myself in what I believed to be my place of refuge since the first day that I moved to Charlottesville. As I sat on the porch of a friend and resident of the public housing site, and listened to her describe what she saw earlier in the day. She described the anarchy and pain that of looking at white people with fire in their eyes intent on hurting and harming everyone that they could find who were different from them. She described the absolute fright that her cousin felt when it was said that a group of armed White Supremacists walked into Friendship Court (another housing development) with automatic weapons with the same fire in their eyes. How people in our community had never heard or seen the things that our grandparents told us about, but this must be it. She asked me what were we going to do?

I told her to stand tall. Part of saying this was for her, part of it was for me. I thought about all of the people who were at the community backpack giveaway. The brothers who I saw defend the park. I thought about the people who were fighting for us in front of the Park. I thought about Dr. West and the clergy who were committed to keeping us safe. We can't give up now. So, I told her again, "...it's going to be ok. *Stand tall...* I promise everything's going to be alright." I couldn't be made a liar, so because of that, it had to be okay. My phone was blowing up, and it was time to go back into the city. It was time to head to the next site. I went to all of our public housing sites that night, and the scenes they described, their sense of the moment were all the same.

I had my promises down. And I meant what I said, and believed every word of it. **We were going to be okay!**

As the night went on, the rain picked up. CNN wanted to do an interview outside in the rain, which I thought was odd, but I agreed. I thought this would be a moment. Not simply because we were going to be on National TV, but it was an opportunity to show the nation that our city might have took a punch in the face, but we weren't going to be knocked out. We were going to come back swinging. We were going to come back stronger and more unified than ever. One of my daughters happened to be in Charlotte, NC that weekend and was flipping through the television while calling me on the phone. I told her that I couldn't talk long, but to turn to CNN because daddy was about to go on soon. We said our regular routine of Daddy loves you, and she's the smartest little bookie butt in the world as I was being mic'd up and positioned.

We hung up the phone and I was mentally being prepared to answer whatever questions were about to be asked, as my phone started ringing profusely. I asked to be excused, and it was my daughter again – who was crying on the other line. She was watching the loops of the media outlets that were showing the driver of the car plowing into the crowd of patrons in our city. She was petrified. She repeatedly said that she thought those people were trying to kill her daddy. It was at that moment that I felt a different sense of weight on my body. I had not seen the news, I had not listened to what the media was saying about what was happening in my city, I was living it. But it was my eight-year old daughter who brought it home for me. Our city looked like a war zone to them and my family believed that I was in immediate danger. My daughter, one of the loves of my life, thought that I was about to die. I took a quick second to reassure her that daddy was ok. In fact, daddy was about to speak on television. I am okay. It was troubling for sure, but this wasn't the time to be afraid. It was the time to show strength. The nation was watching, and to be honest I was more pissed than anything else that these cowards had come to our city and made us look as if they had defeated us. I wanted the world to know that we are unafraid, that we had not lost, and that we would in fact stand tall together.

The interview closed and the rain continued to pour. It stopped, began again, and stopped some more. It reminded me of the city at that time. Rain doesn't last forever; the sun eventually comes out. I called and spoke to my wife and assured her that I was ok. I prayed that night before bed that tomorrow would be a better day.

Sunday, August 13th began around 6:00 AM with calls from family, friends, and people throughout the state. I decided to turn on the television and finally see what was being shown. It literally made me sick to my stomach.

Although it was making us look like a city in shambles, I knew that we had to try and stand firm and show that collectively we were able to overcome this hate. There was a church service in which all of the dignitaries from across the state came to Charlottesville for a service at Mt. Zion First African Baptist Church, one of the most historic churches in our city. While the service was packed with community and media, it was still more to be done. In the community as a whole, actually out in the streets, there was work to be done. I made it a point to be able to go out and walk down every street downtown. People from all over were present, were ready to be vocal, but it appeared that the majority of the White Supremacists and Neo-Nazi members had left, or went into hiding. While people were looking for answers, others were looking for healing, and some were looking for revenge. Rumors were flying left and right about what happened the day before. The city was truly in a place of reckoning. People were now realizing that all of the things that we were saying for over a year and a half, and for some, decades was right all along.

We live in a city/community that is deep rooted in White Supremacy. This was *not* about a statue. The thought of removing a statue didn't make James Fields come to Charlottesville and drive his vehicle into a group of people. This issue has been here before we began talking about the statues. However, the issue was one that was taken in different ways by different people in the city.

After church, I walked all around the city and especially downtown to remind people that things were going to be okay... it was definitely a sobering moment. However, while people downtown were all over the place in regards to their emotional state, just as it was the day before, at Tonsler Park, a different story was playing out. It was the Championship game of the Banks Collage BCBA Men's Basketball league. Nearly 200 people or so were packed at Tonsler Park for the game, and although there was a moment of silence for Heather Heyer, and for many in the park, it was an issue that was separate for them. The threat of White Supremacy attacking them or dealing with the ills of society was something that was the norm. To a certain extent, the feeling amongst those who were on "this side of the tracks" was that we were sorry that this happened, but life goes on. These people were here before August 12, here on August 12, and will be here after August 12th.

As I walked into the park to catch the end of the game, people were asking if I was ok, and if the city was ok. Thy expressed how they were sorry about what happened, but essentially that was it. For many, this wasn't *our* problem. It was an issue that other white people had to fix, because it was white people who created this issue, who thrived and/or gained because of this issue, and were finally feeling what we had felt forever. For now,

179

the basketball game was on, and the local team, the Monstars, led by a young man who was a local business owner and philanthropist, won. Music was blasting throughout the park, champagne flowed and people cheered for their victory. The atmosphere and emotion was joyous, to say the very least.

A couple of miles away, however, the scene/feeling was immensely different.

Grief reigned over downtown and its inhabitants. Hundreds of people gathered on 4th St. to pay their respects to Heather Heyer, and the rest of the victims who had been injured the day before. Many were in a state of disbelief. As I arrived at the vigil, I noticed that the scene was the complete opposite of the one that I had just left. There was little to no talking, mostly tears. As Heather's friends arrived, people rushed to show them love, and it looked as if it were just a mob of people conjuring on them. I had the chance to walk down the street and talk with them, and it's something that I will never forget. There were a few speeches and words were shared by clergy members, a couple of community folks, and a few others. That's not what I'll remember. It was Marcus, a close family friend of Heather and his fiancé as well as Heather's best friends, who stood out most to me. The pain in their eyes, was clear. Marcus and I went down the street and we shared words. I've seen a lot of pain in my day, but the look in his eye was something unlike anything that I had ever seen. He was in a wheelchair, leg broken and fractured. His friend and her

180

friends were still back the next day, in the same spot, not allowing them to be silenced or defeated. Our conversation broke my heart, but also left me feeling that we had embarked on a place that we had never been before. Blood was shed. Lives were lost. Pain was felt. But we were not defeated.

Marcus left me feeling like we had to fight back. We could not allow the White Supremacists to feel as if they won this battle. They did not. We had to fight now, more than ever. As the weekend was coming to an end, it was clear that we had a long road ahead, but it was a necessary road. I've never told Marcus, his wife, or his friends this, but they were the ones that ended the weekend for me. They made me feel like yes, it was tough, and we have a rough road ahead, but we will be better. We have to be. We owe it not only to Heather and the officers who lost their lives, or the people who were hit by the car, or those who were beaten, or those who absolutely have been fighting this fight for generations. We owe them. It was about to get even crazier, but we still owe them. We had to keep pushing.

Chapter 17

The Following Year

The next year was a complete whirlwind. August 11th, 12th, and 13th changed the landscape of the city forever. I am often asked, what changed in the year since the terrorist attacks. The city had been turned upside down, and I'm guessing that Thomas Jefferson was spinning in his grave. Charlottesville had often been known as a city that was one of civility, one that was happy, one that was, for some, utopia. Our city was often known and rated as one of the happiest and the healthiest in the country, a healthy and happy place for all. I remember literally begging friends on social media to come to the city council meeting. I would often see the same 20 or so people at the meeting. It was clear that after the events that our community endured throughout the summer of 2017, the meetings, the city, the direction, the boldness, and everything else would never be the same.

August 21, 2017 - Charlottesville City Council Meeting

In the days after the tragedy, more and more information came to light. Along with the information were a lot of different people's perspectives and point of views about what had happened. The council and the people of the city as a whole, underestimated the pain and damage that the city had undergone. The council chambers were packed. We had a discussion before the meeting about how the meeting should flow, and I was adamant that we should not allow ourselves to go through this particular situation as business as usual. This was a different situation entirely. There was a completely different feeling throughout the city and in no way was I going to allow us to attempt to have a meeting with business items, agenda items, announcements, and awards. I was essentially told that I was wrong, and that we would proceed forward as usual. It was believed that we could show strength by making a brief statement, allowing people to express themselves during the public comment, and then move on. We were wrong.

As soon as the meeting began, it was clear that things were different. The room was reminiscent of the decisions about the statue, but with even more energy in the space. This was the first public meeting since the tragedy and emotions were bound to be high but this was intense - like nothing I had felt before. Shortly after the meeting began, we proceeded with public comment, and it was clear that people were hurting... They were

184

grieving and ready to explode. It was obvious that there were a lot of people who were living with real life PTSD. It was no more than 10 minutes into the public comment section of the meeting before the entire room erupted. The crowd was livid with how the police conducted themselves during the rally, they were livid that they believed that they had warned city council about what was about to happen and were ignored, and many of them were simply traumatized. It was obvious, this was not about to be a regular meeting.

As the public comment period went on, more and more people began to yell from the crowd. When our mayor at the time began to say any word, he was immediately shouted down. This was different from what we saw in the past discussing other controversial topics, as this was real pain erupting up from the bellies of people from throughout the city. Our tone as a City Council as a whole was one that was tone-deaf to be honest. Even in the midst of people clearly hurting and trying their best to deal with what had just transpired, we were looking for calm and civility. In my opinion, just because someone curses or says "a bad word" at a meeting, doesn't mean that they are a bad person. Sometimes passion conveys itself in boundless forms. But the council was looking to maintain order, and I honestly believe that the feeling was that "even though you are upset, there is a certain way to express yourself."

While that may be how *some* people operate, it is ridiculous to expect everyone to be that way.

185

The sheer fact that the council was reluctant to even be open to allowing others to express themselves in a different way set a horrible precedent. In the past, we had members of the public removed during the meetings for outburst, because more times than not their behavior was off putting in the eyes of the majority. Now, people were coming off one of the worst tragedies that we had seen in recent years, and we expected people to be civil? No way. Attempting to have a regular meeting was a huge mistake, and now we were paying for it. The law enforcement or *"sergeant at arms"* was asked to remove three people in the meeting for either shouting out or being "disruptive" which was code for making the Council, as a whole uncomfortable. This set the crowd off in an uproar, as again, it appeared that we were not listening or empathizing. I won't lie, I was a little caught off guard by all of it, but I understood where they were coming from. You can't police people's emotions, and you can't tell people how to feel after a tragedy.

There definitely should have been some extra leeway on this night of all nights. People instantly demanded that the three people be released, and this led to a complete takeover of the meeting. It was clear, this was no regular meeting. People were going to be vocal, and the council was going to either have to cancel the meeting, or face the music. As people yelled and expressed themselves more, another group of younger folks, from what I thought were just college students, rushed the podium with a banner. It read: **"Blood on Your Hands."** It was clear at that time that my colleagues literally wanted to do any and everything but be inside of the City Council chambers, so they retreated to the back portion of the council chambers where the television production for the meeting was located. I decided to stay in the room.

I'm not sure why, but a large part of me empathized and actually felt the exact same way that the protestors did. We all were upset that these idiots came into our city, but to a certain extent, it was plausible to believe that the red carpet was rolled out for them. The passive aggressiveness and moderate attention to the feelings of those who believed that the statues were more than art, but a true ode to White Supremacy was ignored. Two of our councilors, in the eyes of many, made many feel as though the words that we were saying were invalid. In the months prior, myself and several community members spoke at length about the inequities in the city. How things were not as happy and jolly as some so desperately wanted to make it seem. We were not in a time in which things could just be as they were before. The people, yes, the ones who are often forgotten, rarely heard from, or who were often told in a subtle way that they did not matter were now being vocal. And with their voice, spoke up in a major way. There was an awakening, a lot of white people in the community were now willing to lend their voices in support in the need for change. It wasn't just the "young radical" as I heard some people describe it. It was also the moderate and mild toned person who saw the events of the entire summer as a wakeup call. All of these people were in council chambers, and watching the council meeting on television. What on the outside looked like chaos, for me was more so the oppressed finally being heard. It was reminiscent of the mantra coined by Malcolm X, "*By any means necessary.*" that the people were going to be heard. If they had to take over a meeting, they were going to take over a meeting. We, the city council, had an obligation to listen to them, not be afraid of them. We all deserved to take this tongue lashing.

As the people in the crowd chanted and stood, I was in the council chambers chanting with them. I then thought that we couldn't just chant all night, and my colleagues had to come back out. I went in the back where they were and pleaded with them to come back out and literally face the music. I convinced them that we should scrap the meeting and simply have a public hearing for the entire meeting. They all agreed that I should run the public comment portion of it all, because we all knew that literally anytime Mike or Kathy would say anything, people were going to shout them down. I came back out and told the crowd that we were going to listen to them, not fight back, not argue with what they say, but truly listen. Due to the fact that it was literally an overflow of people inside the chambers and even more so in the overflow rooms, we decided that we would allow everyone to get at least one minute to speak without interruption, so that everyone who was there had the chance to speak. Words can't describe the stories that came out of that meeting. The trauma was real. The pain was evident. The scar was one that would be with us for a very long time, if not the rest of our lives. The theme of the meeting in my opinion, was summed up best by Brother Tracy Saxson, a lifelong resident of the city.

"I'm outraged!" said Tracy Saxon, 41. "I watched my people get beat and murdered. They let Nazis in here have freedom of speech, and they protect them? And we can't have freedom of speech?"

It was clear, we had a lot of work to do, and this was going to be a very long and uncomfortable road. After the nearly four hours of public comment, we as a council did something that we should have done months before; While discussing the statue of Robert E. Lee and Lee Park, we decided to bring up another topic that we were essentially ignoring – the larger than life Confederate statue of Stonewall Jackson at Jackson Park which was located literally right outside of the Courthouse downtown. Think about the feeling that a black person would have walking inside of a courtroom, to face a system that continuously denies us our inalienable rights, consistently worked in a manner that was less than equitable, and was a constant reminder that the justice system wasn't for us, while looking at a statue of a Confederate General on a horse. The same Confederacy that fought to keep Black people enslaved, that in its constitution clearly stated that Black people were inferior, and believed that we were no more than the livestock on their plantations. There was a big difference in the vote to remove the statue of Stonewall

Jackson on this date. This vote was unanimous, 5-0. We also agreed to move forward with an independent outside investigation to review what happened on the weekend of August 12th. The sentiment was that we wanted to know where we failed, so that we could be transparent with the community, but also to not make the same mistake that we had before. I can honestly say that if the people did not come out as strong as they did, we may not have pushed ourselves to the limit that we did. It might have been out of guilt, but it happened, and that was a step in the right direction.

Chapter 18

Dealing with An Open Wound

When the television cameras leave and when the NPR reporters and radio interviews stop talking about us, we still have work to do here in Charlottesville. Charlottesville opened the eyes of many, both nationally and locally, but having an eye-opening experience is just the first part of the process. A patient can be diagnosed, but still opt out of the surgery – even when it's recommended. It was my job and the community's job, to not allow our city to opt out of the hard work, regardless of how uncomfortable and difficult that it may be. I remember shortly after the statue discussion feeling like I was on an island. Was kind of feeling like the load was mine to carry, and if I didn't say or do something or be loud and vocal, then the envelope wouldn't have been pushed. Those days were over. It was now more evident than ever, we had several leaders in our community who were willing to push us forward. I may have been the one on the television in the early stages, but now there were more voices being elevated.

My sister in the struggle, Dr. Jalane Schmidt was a professor at the University of Virginia, and a lead

193

organizer in the local Black Lives Matter organization. It's really difficult for an elected official, no matter how "down for the cause" that they may be, to be in all of the different groups that are pushing to change the system. While I may agree with the work that the organization is doing, there still needs to be a level of separation. Dr. Schmidt had been putting in work for a while, and she had been elevated as not only a community leader, but as an information disseminator. There was a new wave of black voices in the community, and it was extremely refreshing. Both young and old, from Zyahna Bryant, to Deacon Don Gathers, to Tanesha Hudson, to Will Jones to Katrina Turner and Rosia Parker, and several others. There was a new crop of vocal and active people who were determined to not allow our community to go back to being the same.

In the midst of the active and constant push for change, there was another homegrown voice that was blossoming in ways that our city had never seen... Nikuyah Walker was running for city council as an Independent, and most people in the city thought that it was a far-gone conclusion that she was a formidable candidate... that there was no way that she could actually win. It had been estimated that nearly 80-85% of the city was Democrat, and once the Democratic primary was over, the city council election was over. This year was different. Nikuyah was a woman who had always been vocal, but in her own way.

She was one of my biggest supporters when the White Supremacists were attempting to attack me and my livelihood in 2016 and 2017. I knew that if she won, it would shake up the entire city. We had never had two African-Americans on our city council in our city's history, and there was a general feeling amongst many in our community that as one person told me at the park, "they ain't going to let two of us get up there. Hell, they barely want one." But the tide was changing. It was a mixture of White Guilt, mixed with the need to do the right thing. The people from the area who had been disenfranchised were speaking up and finding their voice. The surgery was slowly but surely taking place. However, as we all know, change is never easy, and the powers that be, the powers that had been in position of influence for generations were not about to let this kind of change happen easily.

The city council decided to put a shroud over the statues of Robert E. Lee and Stonewall Jackson to pay our respect to those who lost their lives on August 12th. The shroud was intended to symbolize mourning, just as when people wear all black after the death of a loved one. It was our way of mourning as a whole in our city. Because of this though, even after everything that transpired, we were met with hate. It had been a pretty consistent occurrence for me to receive death threats. The school in which two of my daughters attended had a bomb threat earlier in the year. I even had received letters at my home saying how I should be hung, or how people were going to come to my house and shoot me in the face, and we had a couple of hiccups here and there at my house with people riding by and saying different things while speeding away. I had and still do just believe that this is what comes with the work of trying to create change. However, for my family, it was different. My wife and children moved to Charlottesville shortly after we were married in 2016. This was a whole new experience for them. They had no other family members present, few people who they knew, and were in a completely different cultural environment than what they were accustomed to. Even in all of that, they had to endure the hate that came our way collectively. It ate at me, and it still does for a variety of reasons.

Now, it was not only me and my family dealing with it, the bigots and those who opposed us were being creative. The local government as a whole was being sued left and right, and the people in the community who were fighting for change were now also being targeted. More stories were coming out about the Nazi's that were still in the area, about those who actually lived amongst us. There was a narrative that was being pushed far and wide that the people who came to our community were all outsiders, but that's not entirely true. Our community as a whole, both the city, the county and the surrounding areas were hotbeds for racists. These individuals were not the ones that were the obvious people who you could point out. Many of the White Supremacists that were among us were those who practiced covert White Supremacy and benefited from the advantages of subtle racism. We saw many of them come out in 2016 after the

196

statue debate, and even more so after election of "45." Those were the ones who were bold and, in our face, and vowed to keep Charlottesville, and Virginia as a whole what it had always been. A place where their heritage, lineage, and race reigned supreme.

After August 12th, as more people of all races became more vocal about speaking out for equity, the ugliness came out once again. People were being followed. Churches and Synagogues were targeted during August 12th but also in the months after the event. The groups that decided to speak out were now targets. The people who decided to stand up, were not only praised for their bravery, but also had to face the hate.

The hate didn't stop there. The targeting didn't just magically end. This was deep rooted, and even though a tragedy had taken place, didn't mean that people were just going to magically be transformed and understand our perspective. In fact, it appeared that the more people who decided to become allies, the more lawsuits ensued. We were sued by a group of people who wanted the statues to be uncovered, and for the names of the parks to be reverted back to the names of Confederate Generals with the actual statues remaining exactly where they were. The council was challenged by a variety of people who believed that the death of Heather Heyer, the State Troopers, and the unrest as a whole was all of our fault. Most of these same people further insisted that this was specifically my fault since I was the one who was so vocal about the statues being moved. The issue was

197

that this was not about the statues. It wasn't even about the tragedy that took place. It was more so about people feeling uncomfortable with the fact that what they thought about the place that they grew up, and even themselves was being challenged. To that point, the people who were being vocal and challenging the systems were growing in number. The sentiment of the city as a whole was changing. The council meetings were now more attended than they've ever been. The very thing that many of us were hoping for in regards to community engagement was happening. People were taking control of the process, and it wasn't the people who were traditionally in positions of power. The new climate, the desire for change, the push for truth and accountability was the perfect storm for our November 2017 election. The unthinkable took place, Nikuyah Walker, a home grown African-American Woman became the first Independent candidate since 1948 to be elected to Charlottesville City Council.

She literally shocked much of the traditionalists in our community, and proved that the days of yesteryear as it pertained to Charlottesville were done. Nikuyah had beaten out the field, that also included Amy Laufer, a well renowned member of the party and was the Chairman of the local School board. The threat of having two black people on City Council was no longer a dream, but a nightmare for some, and something that a lot people in the community thought would never happen. Shortly before Nikuyah was elected she created a buzz around the city like no other. She was and still is an unapologetically black, incredibly intelligent and thorough, warrior. While in the midst of what saw as chaos in our city, she was able to bring about a new level of energy. This would not come easy though, as even in our new climate, she was met by traditionalists who were afraid of her and her message.

Literally two days before the election, the Daily Progress published an article on the front page essentially labeling her as the "Angry Black Woman." Yes, the same Daily Progress that published an Editorial one day before the August 12 tragedy blaming me for the entire Unite the Right rally and coded in racist and bigoted language, used a similar tactic to paint Nikuyah in the same light two days before her election. To say that I was livid would be an understatement. This however though, was a part of our city's awakening. The scab was slowly being pulled off. I had been warned in so many ways by the local Democratic Party that Nikuyah was an independent, that it was noticeable that I rarely attended any local party events for the two people who won the Democratic nomination, and I was often seen with Nikuyah, therefore, many in the party wondered where my loyalty rested. The tone/suggestion of those conversations coupled with the article that was published in the paper really set me off. I ended up publishing my own response in defense of Nikuyah with hopes that she knew, as well as the community as a whole understood that we had to start sticking up for each other. This was a part of the changing of the guard. Nikuyah went on to win the election, and it was a major shock to some, and a pleasant surprise to others. Nikuyah couldn't win this race with only the Black vote. She had to be able to bring in the entire community for this. She did. It was a clear sign that we were in new times. While we knew that our city was changing, that we were in new and unchartered territory, and that things were not quite the same, it was still hard to tell. Yes, we had more people at the city council meetings, more people being vocal, but that was on the surface. However, after the election, it was clear that people of all persuasions were sick and tired of being sick and tired. History was now made!

This was part of the of the awakening!

Chapter 19

Surgery On An Open Wound

I t felt like everything that we did from August 12th, 2017 was leading up to August 12th, 2018. Within a year, we had a new mayor, a new city attorney, a new police chief, a new city manager, and a new city. The culture was different. Our citizens demanded more from us, and they expressed their desire for change every opportunity that they could. City Council meetings were no longer quiet and quaint like they were when I first joined. They were now full of action, people being vocal, and in some instances, recesses had to be called due to the crowd expressing themselves in ways that stopped us from conducting the business portion of the meeting. The change that our city was undergoing in real time however was painful for many throughout the city. Think about it - we were now not only dealing with a national tragedy, but we were also dealing with people who had been in Charlottesville their entire lives, who rarely talked about race in real and transparent ways...

I cannot express enough how many times I've been told;

"I've been here my entire life, and race was never a problem. Now that you've come along, it feels like our city has turned into a race war. This is all your fault."

For a very long time, those words were difficult for me to hear, but over time, I realized that these were the growing pains that were necessary for our city to grow. Charlottesville is the type of city that was content with being what we were. A small, sweet, gentle, and polite, but also racist city. It's easy to practice gentle racism. It's the kind that cuts you and smiles in your face. We now had not one, but two, "Race Baiting Radicals" in our office who were intent on showing our community the ugly wounds of the past and present, and forcing us to do the necessary work to be better.

Nikuyah officially became Madame Mayor at the first meeting in January, which made our city council chambers erupt in happiness, and it again, put the rest of our city on notice. This was a new day. What was also evident was that we, as a council, were not going to operate like those from years prior. We were going down the road to transparency. Since our City Council only has five members, we are all at large, and have a weak mayor-city manager style of government. At the time, I was in the Vice Mayor position, and many thought that I would just transition into the role of mayor. I can't lie, I did initially want to be mayor, but there was just something that I thought was off about it. At this point I was getting more national attention than I deserved, my wife and I wanted to spend more time together, and I continuously thought about my three daughters. How dope would it be if they could see a black woman as mayor of the same city that Thomas Jefferson once ruled? I made my mind up about two hours before the meeting and was content that this is what needed to be done. We were in a peculiar position in our city. For the first time ever, we had more than one African-American on City Council. For the first time since 1948 we had an Independent in a chair. Now, we had to see if we could make more history.

So, when we on City Council began the discussion of who would be the next mayor, I made the initial remarks. In essence, history means a lot to me, but making history means even more. We had the chance to make history with Nikuyah, and we all needed to support her in becoming the mayor. We all had a pivotal moment to move towards righting our wrongs, not only from the initial split vote on the statues, or how we handled August 12, but to make a symbolic gesture that we were listening to the public. The crowd was rather appreciative, but all of my colleagues were not. We had three nominees for mayor. I nominated Nikuyah, Kathy Galvin nominated herself, and Nikuyah nominated me, which I turned down. This was her time, and I wanted her to shine. After much deliberation, we officially made Nikuyah the mayor on a 4-1 vote. It was absolutely uncommon for council to have this discussion publicly, as these things were usually always sorted out behind closed doors. We had made history though, and I was already pushing for more.

I wanted us to have two African-Americans in the position with Nikuyah as Mayor and me serving as Vice-Mayor. While I knew that both positions were simply ceremonial and only held a title, the symbolism mattered. A black Mayor and Vice Mayor in Charlottesville? People thought it would never happen. In fact, that was my motivation. I was having a discussion the week before with Mr. Eugene Williams, an African-American legend in our community with ties back to desegregating the schools, building affordable housing, and most infamously known for - being the former NAACP president in Charlottesville.

He said to me very plainly, "Them White folks ain't going to let both of yall be mayor and vice mayor. We ain't getting two." Now Mr. Williams was almost 90 years old, and while he blazed a path in Charlottesville, he still believed that there was a certain barrier in our community. I desperately wanted to prove him wrong, but in the end, he was right.

While we didn't get a Black Mayor *and* Vice Mayor, we did get two women as Mayor and Vice Mayor with Heather Hill now assuming my old position. For me, it wasn't a big deal, we got the one that we wanted. The stage was also set now like never before. We meant business, and things were not going to be the same.

206

Dr. Wes Bellamy

Chapter 20

The New Loud Voice of Charlottesville

Charlottesville, in my opinion, is and will always be, Ground Zero for the Awakening. While across the country there have been many initiatives and narratives to promote new voices, our city was struggling with the fact that new people were at the table. It was more than common to hear from members of the community, both black and white and young and old say, "I have never seen the city like this." For most, that was supposed to be some kind of reprimand, but in my opinion, it was a good thing. Many of them were right. They had never seen people in the community demanding the kind of accountability that many were calling for. They had never seen people show such passion and express themselves with words that were in the dictionary and words that were common in the street at a city council meeting. In recent history, there was never a time in which there was such turnover within major parts of the city. This too changed my life. Our police chief was gone. Our City Manager was gone. Our City Attorney was gone. Our Communications Director was gone. Our Public Works Director was gone.

Our Clerk of City Council was gone. The President of the University of Virginia was gone. Two of the City Councilors who were in office during 2017 were gone.

Many of the voices that were accustomed to coming to the city council meetings were replaced with a new crowd. The city was changed, for better or for worse –

we were and are different.

There was also something else that was moving throughout our city… a strong push to elevate the voices of Black Women. A strong push to mobilize and organize. A grand push to not allow things to go back to being the same. Throughout all of this, a new crop of leaders and groups were developing, and the tension was evident.

While Nikuyah was a force to be reckoned with as Mayor, she pushed her agenda for equity and transparency in ways that it had never been done in our communit. She was joined by other black Women like Zyahna Bryant, or little Fannie Lou Hammer as I like to call her, Lisa Woolfolk, Dr. Jalane Schmidt, Dr. Andrea Douglas, Tanesha Hudson, Yolunda Harrell, Yolonda Coles-Jones, and several others were stepping in and speaking up in the same way that other matriarchs of the past had done. We all were familiar with local activists and organizers like Joy Johnson, who was a fierce advocate, who I affectionately refer to as Auntie.

We were familiar with Audrey Toliver and Deidra Gilmore, who had put themselves on the line while fighting for people in low income housing for decades. We were familiar with our hero, Dr. Holly Edwards, who passed away in January 2017, and was the last Black City Councilor prior to me coming into office. However, we were now seeing that Black women were speaking out, being vocal, and finally getting the respect that they deserved. While this may seem like something small and trivial in comparison to other cities, we have to keep in mind the context of our city and our community. The same place where Thomas Jefferson raped his Black slaves and had children with Sally Hemmings, and then for hundreds of years, the area acted as if it was an unfounded rumor that was not to be discussed at the dinner table. The same place that for decades denied the rights and failed to respect black women, now had to listen to them.

Reverend Barbara Brown-Grooms, who had been a fierce advocate for civil rights in our community for decades, was finally, in my opinion, getting her just due. It was not just the black voices who were being vocal that were being recognized. The University of Virginia, which has often been viewed as the Good Ole Boys Club for white men, sent shockwaves throughout the community when they decided to bring in Carla Williams, the University's first ever Black Female Athletic Director. As I look back on this past year, I think long and hard about how difficult this transition has been for many. We have been coming to grips with the fact that much of what we were doing

211

in years past is outdated, and we must move forward collectively and adjust to what is needed for times such as the present. Our last police chief, Al Thomas, was a friend of mine, was forced to take on an unfair amount of blame for the August 12th attack. Yes, tactical mistakes were made and different things could have been done, but we all played a role in what was one of the largest White Supremacists' gatherings in our generation. Because of this, Chief Thomas and ourselves brought in a dynamic, thorough, thoughtful, and strategic woman of color to make even more history.

We not only hired our city's first female police chief, but she was the first woman of color to hold the position. We didn't hire Chief Brackney because she was a woman of color, however, we hired her because we saw that she brought ought something to the table that we had never seen before. Her hire, as well as the other aforementioned hires, would have never happened before. This community was rooted in tradition, and that was changing. I think it's something that as we are living in it, we don't quite recognize, but in the year since the August 12th attack, I have seen the barriers of different voices due to patriarchic nonsense be broken down like the Berlin Wall.

I'm often asked what's changed in our city over the past year… Well, a lot. But this change didn't just start on August 12th, 2017, it's been brewing for a while, we are now just starting to reap the benefits of it all. During this time, I was also learning to grow. I was beginning to learn that accountability and transparency looks different in the eyes of different people with different perspectives.

As our city was growing, we were all being forced to look ourselves in the mirror and truly think about what was going on in our city. White Supremacy was only one issue, but affordable housing, health disparities, a tech and digital divide, an education gap, and wealth disparities also existed. This new group of vocal leaders and activists were pushing our city in a direction that forced us to deal with these things, not later, but right now. When I presented the equity package in 2016, it was with the hope that it would change the playing field through policy. When we began to talk about the need for equitable policing in our communities years ago, it was with the hope that things would change sooner rather than later. However, I learned that for many, if something isn't constantly talked about, very few will understand what is going on to be changed. The new tactic was to be as vocal as possible at all times. There would no longer be a feeling as if one's voice is being suppressed and stifled. If that meant yelling and cursing at a meeting, then so be it.

We saw a new wave of decorum not only in our city council chambers, but throughout the city as a whole. Protestors and activists alike took to the streets, to online platforms, to the media, and to wherever they wanted to go to demand that they no longer would allow for the days of old to be continued. They were adamant that they wanted change, justice, and equity, and they

213

were not about to wait on empty promises about how it would come later, they wanted it now. Just as 45 empowered the racists and supremacists to come out of the woodworks, he had also woke up a new wave of people who were sick and tired of being sick and tired. A new wave of people who realized that their privilege had taken them to heights that they had taken for granted. We were now in a city in which was put on notice. We all didn't have to understand it or agree with it, but it was happening. One way or another. I saw planning commission meetings being taken over, I saw protestors taking to the street, I saw activists winning seats, I saw boards and commissions changing, I saw... an awakening.

No Matter What We Do, We Have to Get August 12th Right – The One Year Anniversary and the Aftermath

The lead-up to the one-year anniversary was much different from what we experienced the year before. While we were waking up as a community, the change in all of it was painful. There was still a great deal of anxiety in 2018, but this time it was different. In 2017, there was a fear of the unknown. We had an idea of what may happen but we weren't quite sure, because it hadn't happened yet. In 2017 there was still a feeling from many in our community that Charlottesville was a quiet, quaint place that couldn't possibly be infiltrated with White Supremacists, both homegrown, local, or from elsewhere. There was no way that we had serious racial issues here. That was a feeling that was shared by those in disbelief that race was still an issue locally. It wasn't until they physically witnessed the tragedy in real time or watched it online or on a television screen did, they understand the magnitude of the issues at hand. There were also a group of people who were willing and ready to defend our city at all cost from racist bigots. In the aftermath of all of this, one year later we saw a community that was empowered and awakened in many ways, but also very much so traumatized.

Our city as a whole wanted so desperately to get this right, that everyone was on edge in the months leading up to the one-year anniversary of the tragedy in our community. This time around the planning began much earlier. The attention to detail in regards to the planning was different. More community meetings were held. The concerns of the activists, the protestors, the community members, and the citizens of the city as a whole was much different. The collaboration between law enforcement and local and state government was much better. One other thing was also working in our favor, we had a year to prepare and learn from our prior mistakes, and we were dealing with a much weaker opponent in the Far-Right White Supremacists from the year before. In my opinion, it's really difficult to place all of the blame of the weekend of August 12th, 2017 on one person or in one place. No community had ever been through what we went through. While we were seeing a variety of threats and people saying a lot of different things online and social media, and personally I was getting a lot of death threats and people saying they were going to do this or that to me, it's difficult to know how much of it is real, and how much of it is some guy sitting in the basement of his mother's house being a thumb thug and pretending his twitter fingers are trigger fingers.

We learned in 2017 that the community was right in a lot of what they were saying. Overall, A12 was one of the most shocking days in recent American history. Fast forward to 2018, essentially new staff and leadership throughout, a year to analyze mistakes and mishaps, and an organizer who had essentially been exiled from almost all of his racist and White Supremacists followers, and well... that creates a very different situation.

Nonetheless, it was imperative that whether or not Jason Kessler was coming to our community or not, we needed to be prepared for the worst. This made many feel as if the city and local government and law enforcement was looking to make up for the lack of protection the year before. My personal answer to them would be yes, they were correct.

216

Whether or not that was the right thing to do, history will be the judge.

The month of August, 2018 was a big one for Charlottesville. Not only was our staff and community partners preparing for the worst possible scenario, we had to deal with a public that wasn't sure about what was going to happen.

Jason Kessler was still pushing forward with a lawsuit against the city to be able to have his Unite the Right rally at the same park where the mayhem of the year before took place. He was adamant that he had every right to do so, and just as he did the year before, was taking the city to Federal Court to be able to have his rally. In one of the most bizarre things that I ever witnessed, on the day of the hearing, Kessler decided initially not to show up, his attorney arrived late, and then after very brief opening statements, Kessler arrived to the Federal Court only to say that he was withdrawing his application for a permit. After months of work by our in-house city attorney and other law firms who had decided to help us pro-bono, the issue of whether or not Kessler was coming was over in less than an hour.

Kessler in a later statement said that he was turning all of his attention to Washington, D.C. where he had obtained a permit to have a rally earlier in the summer. The mood in our city was one of both relief and an underlying level of uncertainty. Some people thought that this was some kind of trick, and Kessler was playing a game with our city. Others thought that this meant that we were in the clear. I honestly didn't know what to believe. Our police chief and city manager both agreed that we should move forward with the plans at hand, and be prepared for the absolute worst-case scenario.

There was also concerns of a lone wolf attack or someone coming to our city to try and make a name for themselves by doing something horrific on the weekend of the anniversary, so the police and city leaders were committed to maintaining the public's safety at all cost. Our current Governor, Ralph Northam, had been in communication with us and it was decided to declare a State of Emergency. While we were not sure of what Kessler was going to do since he withdrew his application for the permit, we still had a city to protect.

In the weeks leading up to August 12th several community meetings took place in an effort to try and bring about a collective understanding of the plans for the weekend. Press releases went out with a list of banned items on the Downtown Mall, road closures, and screenings to get into certain

218

segments of the city, there was a new feeling in the city. One that made many people feel like they were being over policed. It was an incredibly difficult position to be in, and while I understood wholeheartedly why it had to happen, I still understood why people were feeling as if they were being held captive in their own city. It was a much different energy in the city in 2018. My friends and family were concerned that someone was going to try and harm my wife and I in some form or fashion, so there was that element to deal with. Even while assuring them that things were going to be ok, I was secretly saying to them what I actually wanted to believe... *We are going to be fine. Positive energy only. Let's make it through the weekend.*

The media rained down on our community unlike any time before. Our city has become a hashtag, and not in a good way. I couldn't help but feel apprehension as I saw the people who only thought of us as some kind of spectacle came and prodded those who were still dealing with trauma, asked questions and obtained answers from people who were still dealing with their own issues from last year, and sensationalized what was going on. I saw some paint our city in the worst possible light while ignoring all of the progress that had been made over the past twelve months. That Friday, I gave a talk in Washington D.C. about where our community was. As I looked at the crowd, it really hit me how many white people throughout the country, not just in Charlottesville, were coming to grips with what was transpiring. The conversation on the panel was enlightening as I listened to people talk at length about the need for us all to be accountable and accept responsibility for where we were in this country. It was easy to blame the 45th President, but accepting accountable for the roles that we play in aiding and abetting covert and overt racism was also key.

In the 12 months since August 2017 I had literally been around the country and throughout the world talking about what happened and listening to others. It was clear, that the phenomenon that happened in our city changed was more than a moment in time but also changed our country. While I knew that we were gearing up for a hectic weekend, I was proud of what was happening.

The awakening was here.

Upon arriving back in Charlottesville, I skipped out on the church service and gathering for the community, and chose to hang out in one of the public housing sites. It was there, as I've said before, that I felt at home. It was almost a surreal moment, some were actually having a cookout, others were listening to music and winding down from a long week. The issue that *they* were now dealing with was one that we had been dealing with since we came to this country. We knew that we would survive one way or another. Upon leaving, and going home, the Mayor and I were talking on the phone and she made it clear that this night was going to be a calm one. We had nearly 800 police officers from across the state in the city. To some it was excessive, to others it was necessary. To me, it was what it what it was, I just wanted a peaceful night.

Saturday August 11th was shaping up to be a day of the unknown. I woke up and went and played basketball just like I did every Saturday morning at 7:00 AM. My wife and I had breakfast with a couple of friends. I was monitoring social media like a hawk, receiving updates from our city staff, did a couple of interviews, and was riding around the city. The mood and energy had shifted from Charlottesville vs. White Supremacists to some people from Charlottesville vs. the Police. I can't stress how traumatizing it was for some people to see the mere image of police officers on the same streets where a year earlier they had been in one of the craziest times of their lives?

Since our plans for safety were now different, the narrative was one that we were being overhanded and trying to make up for the mishaps of the year before. While for some that was valid, it was a combustible situation that could turn bad at any moment for all. Nonetheless, people were trying their best to keep their cool, exercise their first amendment right to free speech, and the police were trying to simply maintain safety. Everything was cool until the students of the University of Virginia decided to have a rally on the grounds (what most places call campus) that Saturday evening. After having lunch with friends earlier in the day, my wife and I and few other Black couples agreed to go and check out Spike Lee's Black Klansman movie that evening. I told my wife that we needed to stop by UVA for a quick moment first, and she made me promise we wouldn't be there all night. Upon arriving on the grounds to walk to the gathering, the mood was eerie. Police in military gear were everywhere and the campus was completely empty.

As we got closer to the protest, we could feel the tension in the air. We saw a few friends and listened to one of the speakers when out of nowhere, nearly 100 police officers in riot gear showed up in formation nearly 500 feet from us. Admittedly, even when I saw and heard the officers my adrenaline began to pump and I was somewhat alarmed, as I had no idea what was going on. Things were peaceful, so I wasn't sure why the need for the police officers to show up in that manner was necessary. The students and community members who were present were visibly upset and began to move towards the officers. As I walked over to find out what was going on, things started to get chaotic.

I asked to speak to the commanding officer, and was pointed in the direction of whom I needed to speak with. I was informed in a very polite manner that the officers were only there for the protection of the students and community members and the property of the University. We had a conversation about how it could be perceived that showing up in riot gear could lead some people to think otherwise, and he agreed. My brother Don Gathers, a local activist and deacon at our church, joined in the conversation, and the commanding officer decided to inform his officers to lower their shields take a more relaxed position as a peaceful offering of sorts for the community. The situation went from super intense to everyone essentially leaving the area. I breathed a sigh of relief and thanked the officer for his willingness to listen and communicate. We both left that night feeling like we had avoided something that was going to leave us all more divided. Instead, we earned a small victory.

As the students and protestors marched through the city, they actually had a few police escorts. From

223

the University of Virginia up to our Downtown Mall, students and protestors chanted, marched, and for the most part had a peaceful night. As my wife and I came out of the movie, we saw the ending of what appeared to be a good night. We were 2/3rds of the way to a peaceful weekend, but Sunday was August 12th, and the mere pain of that day was enough to scare us all.

The morning of A12 began similar to as it did a year earlier, with a church service. The Reverend Al Sharpton came to Mt. Zion First African Baptist Church, and delivered one of the best sermons that I had ever heard in my life. He spoke about the will to continue to push forward and fight the good fight, and even stuck around to take pictures with every person who wanted one at the service. He also did one of the realist things that I had ever witnessed from someone of his stature. We had been talking during the week about getting together with some of the youth that I work with through We Code, Too and spending some time with them after the service. Unfortunately, his plans changed and he had to get to D.C., but he didn't want to disappoint. After taking pictures with them all, he paid for each one to go to dinner, and made us promise to not go anywhere cheap. The kids loved it, and I really respected the gesture.

224

The day was starting off well, and now it was time to eat. Unfortunately, things would take a turn for the worst. While ordering food and laughing with the kids and the family, I began to get phone calls to get to 4th St. and the memorial site of Heather Heyer ASAP. I apologized to everyone and went on my way, not really knowing what to expect. I said a prayer, listened to some Kendrick Lamar and just hoped for the best, but expected the worst.

Upon arrival, I saw that I was entering a stand-off of sorts. Heather Heyer's mother, Susan Bro, who for the record is one of the coolest people on the planet and has an All-Time invite to the Cookout pass, was having a moment at the space where her daughter lost her life. It was preplanned to allow her and her family to enter and leave without any issues. The problem was that we didn't quite communicate that with everyone else who was there to mourn the same way. After allowing people to come in and out of the area as long as they went through the checkpoint, officers were now not allowing people to enter the memorial area. This made some people upset as they believed that the police were trying to mess with them and stop them from grieving. It was really just miscommunication, but it didn't help that several officers were dressed in riot gear, military tanks were on site, and it looked in the eyes of an everyday person, like a war zone. It was now my task to help this situation deescalate, and to simply try and be a peacemaker and mediator.

As I had done the day before, I asked to speak to the commanding officer, who was very polite, and explained that they needed to keep the area clear for Mrs. Bro. After she left, there were a couple other instances in which things became very tense, but both sides were able to work together to create an amicable solution. It was very different from the year before, as from my point of view, we all had the same goal this year, but the trauma and pain from the year before led to a completely different energy.

At one point, when it was made clear by the officers that people needed to move back due to the officers trying to get control of the area, we were facing a full-blown stand off and shouting match with community members yelling at the police officers. In my opinion, again, it wasn't that people were being anti-police, they were just expressing their frustration with the lack of communication from our end about what was going on. The emotions of the anniversary in addition to it just being a really hot day with people everywhere, didn't help the equation. My saving grace came in the form of Lisa Woolfolk, a resourceful, compassionate, and intelligent sister from the community who worked with the officers, myself, and the Clergy Collective to diffuse the situation between the officers and the community members and activists. After what felt like hours, which probably was actually just a few minutes, things finally calmed down. The officers disbanded and moved to other parts of the area, the activists and community members calmed down and disbursed and we avoided another potential situation that nobody wanted.

I left that event feeling like we had accomplished a weekend that wasn't perfect, but was nowhere near what we experienced the year before. I wrote this on Instagram the morning after:

August 12, 2018 - One Year Later - I have a lot of thoughts and feelings. This weekend was tough emotionally and psychologically. I feel like we all will have our own interpretations of this weekend, but this picture sums up my weekend. It was a weekend in which safety was placed over convenience. It was a weekend of the community coming together in different ways (peaceful protests, community sing outs, chants and rally's, trying to have normalcy by doing what you normally do, and church services with special guests). While I participated in all of the above...most of my time was spent with the people in the street and the police. Protestors and people in the street feeling like the policing that they saw this year was what was needed last year. Some feeling like this is too much. Some feeling like they're not in the city that they love. Police feeling like they have to do their job. Many told me that they necessarily didn't "want" to be here, as they, like all of us, would prefer that no tragedy ever happened in the first place, and this wouldn't be needed. * *

My wife reminded me of how I was at 19,20,21 and what would I be doing if I was that age today. It was an honest question, And I know I would have been protesting like everyone else. But today, at the ripe age of 31 (insert joke here) and in this position, it's different. This weekend I learned that it's possible to be both an activist at heart, and a mediator in action. It's possible to understand the passion of wanting the system to change so bad that you're willing to yell, fight, scream, curse and everything else to release the rage from being tired from being sick and tired..and STILL want to maintain some form of peace, some form of safety, some form of finding the medium between two parties who essentially want the same thing, just in different ways. Our community is hurting. Our community is also healing. This is all part of the process. I'm proud of my city. We aren't perfect, but we are ground zero for the awakening! We are vocal, we are pushing for equity, we are challenging ourselves to be better, and it isn't pretty...but at least we are doing it. #NewCville

Chapter 21

#NewCVille

We were now in a community that was much less concerned with decorum and civility and more concerned with making sure that people were listened to and heard. We were much less concerned with making sure that those who were in positions of influence, authority, had the option to speak or be present because of their status or last name. We no longer cared if they were comfortable. Now we were pushing to ensure that we did everything through an equitable lens. That is still yet a difficult and challenging task. One that requires tears, jeers, and people from a variety of viewpoints feeling frustrated because the change that they want to see, or don't want to see, isn't happening fast enough. All in all, as a city our priorities as a whole have now shifted, and it's no longer a place in which we concern ourselves with the status quo. Charlottesville has been moving in the right direction for some time now, and A12 took us from driving at a 25-mph pace to 75 mph pace.

The change in speed alone is a lot to deal with, but now imagine that if your grandmother was in the car without her seatbelt because she never had to wear one because she only traveled to the local grocery store, school house, and city hall to pay her bills and back. Now the car that she has been accustomed to is on a high-speed highway, and while she wants to get to the destination, it's the speed of the trip that scares her the most. While grandma is in the car, the grandson behind the wheel feels like all of the other cars (cities) are passing him on the interstate. He feels compelled to keep up, and continues to push a little faster, and a little faster, and then tests the car just a little bit more. He wants to tell grandma that he's driving now, and she needs to put on her seatbelt, because they have somewhere to be. But he also realizes that to drive this car, this fast is already pushing it, and to drive it any faster right now, to the chagrin of his own feelings, may mess up the car long term. So, although he may be able to go just a little faster, he must find a steady pace if he wants to get to his destination and not crash before he gets there.

This is how I feel about my position in this city. And I've learned more driving this car than I ever would have studying the traffic signs and laws in a driver's license book.

Becoming Comfortable with Being Uncomfortable:

So, now that my stories been told and all of the facts have been placed onto the table for your consideration... You may be wondering what have I personally learned over the past 2 years...

I think the past 24 months have accelerated my growth as a man and human being like no other. I can still think about the feelings of being so passionate about something that I felt like screaming, lashing out, and telling anyone who disagreed with me to jump off a cliff. I can remember being so judgmental that if you didn't see something exactly as I did, you had to be wrong, and there was no way that you were down with the movement. I remember feeling like that if you weren't willing to sacrifice everything that you possibly could, you were not down with the movement. I think back to the early conversations surrounding the statues, and people who I trusted, warning me that this was a big deal. That I needed to be sure, because although I was not the first person to talk about moving the statues, I would surely become the face of it, and in return, receive the large bulk of the backlash. I remember the calls to my phones from people saying that they were going to hang me, or kill me. I remember the items coming into the mail with my wife's name on them, with my daughter's names on them, or the people riding by trying to scare or intimidate us. I remember thinking about how isolated I felt on City Council being the only person under the age of 40, the only black man, and feeling like the pressure was mine to bear, and to bear alone. I remember thinking about the Klu Klux Klan picking my wedding anniversary to pay a visit to our city and having to choose between spending it with my wife or being in the fray. I think about the feeling of disappointment and shame that I had when I had to tell my students at Albemarle High School that I wasn't coming back. I remember the looks on the faces of the young men in my school that I worked with feeling as if I had given up on them. I remember thinking that this fight for equity was going to cost me everything, and in the end, not much would ever change.

I remember feeling depressed. Feeling out of touch. Feeling like I couldn't be regular or normal anymore. Feeling like my life was in danger. Feeling like just as Colin Kaepernick's decision to kneel during the National Anthem was not about disrespecting the flag, but about racial equity and justice within the criminal justice system, our desire in Charlottesville to create change and push for equity was never about the removal of Confederate Statues or memorials, but about a city and community addressing and dealing with the ills of the past and

234

our desire to make all feel welcome and receive equity. The frustration with having to explain that repeatedly and people pretending that they didn't get it was truly becoming overwhelming. The feeling that I always had to smile no matter what was becoming unbearable. The feeling that maybe all of this was for not, and we should just leave the damn statues alone. I'm being sued individually, the city is being sued left and right, some have lost their limbs, some have lost their lives, others have lost their minds. The consistent tweets, and social media messages and direct messages blaming me for it all was taking a toll on my wife and I. I was thinking that maybe the city and my family would be better off if I just decided to take my life. If I wasn't here, maybe there would be no one else to blame, or the attention could be shifted elsewhere. Maybe then, things could go back to the way that even some of the older Black folks would tell me that they wanted it to be. Maybe then, Charlottesville could move on. And even in those darkest times, the desire to create change superseded any and all negativity.

Because this wasn't about a statue, we had to continue to push forward. I began to shift my focus from protesting on the city council to looking to effect and change policy. If we were ever going to create change in this city, we had to not only push from the outside, but also from within. Changing the landscape of a city is not a one-person job. Creating equity and opening the eyes of people who have been stuck in their own ways for generations does not happen overnight. This, just like my life as a whole, would require growth, and most of all patience. I had to come to the realization that I was not the savior of this community. I was not placed here to lead a one man show and do everything my own way, nor did I have to be involved in every small aspect of change that was taking place. If Charlottesville was going to go to the next level, we had to do it together. We had to be willing to listen to each other.

Moving forward, we have to be willing to bend a little and value the input of those that we disagree with, and use our talents to break down the barriers that have plagued us for hundreds of years. Shortly after August 12th, I decided to make a conscious decision to focus more on policy than protesting. I think about how change is often slower than molasses as we say down south, and as the city was changing, so was I. The quick temper was slowly moving towards patience. I began to focus less on protesting and more on policy. It became evident to me that the Equity Package of 2017 would be the thing that changed more lives than any single word that I could yell from the street. The position from the Equity Package that led to the creation of a

236

position for Black Male Achievement, was filled by a brother named Daniel Fairley, who's been doing outstanding work to break down the negative stigmas around Black men and boys in our community. The money that was put in the equity package for Public Housing Redevelopment led to beginning phases of the Housing Authority being able to solicit partners to create and execute plans for public housing redevelopment.

Early in 2018, I brokered a deal with Ting Internet services to provide High Speed Fiber Optic internet for every single Public Housing resident in the city of Charlottesville. I was able to convince my colleagues on city council to allocate $150,000 pay for all of the installation and hardware costs for each unit so that we could begin to close the digital divide and provide this service to those in need. I think about the push to get a Minority Business Task Force to be adopted to look at the development of African American and other Minority businesses created. I think about how a year later, both of those pushes are paying dividends, as council agreed to hire two new positions to help booster minority businesses and help encourage/educate current minority businesses on how to obtain contracts with the city and others. This comes as people would come to the city council meeting and voice their displeasure openly about the lack Black businesses in our community. We are now doing something about it. I think about how affordable housing has been one of the hottest topics in our community, and the lack of people of color who were born and raised here, had their own businesses and houses stripped from them via Urban Renewal, and now are seeing our community being gentrified. Due to this, myself, our current Mayor Nikuyah Walker, the Public Housing Association of Residents, and other concerned community members are pushing for the city to float a $50 million-dollar bond to completely redevelop all of our public housing sites and create more affordable housing for those below the various Annual Median Income levels designated by the Federal government, in an effort to initiate a bold new strategy to create change in our city. I look around at the Civilian Review Board and the members from the activist community who are strongly pushing for police accountability, and I see change. I look at how now in our community, the topic of race, equity, and making things right are usually at the forefront of nearly every conversation that is taking place on both a macro and micro level in our community.

Our schools have adjusted their policies and curriculum to discuss race and history in a more truthful way. Coming off the heels of the Blue Ribbon Commission from the initial statue discussion in 2016, we were able to allocate $1 million to tell the full story of race and reconciliation in our community. In the summer of 2018, again on my wedding anniversary, our city made a new memory for my wife and I. We kicked off a six day "Cville Pilgrimage" with 100 people (Black, White, Latino, Young, Seasoned, Baptist, Catholic, Atheist, rich, poor, and indifferent) from Charlottesville and Albemarle County looking to learn more about the history of lynchings, Jim Crow, the Civil Rights movement, and just how far we have come, and how much further we have to go in regards to race relations in our community and throughout the south. The trip was led by Dr. Andrea Douglas of the African American Heritage Center, and Dr. Jalane Schmidt of the University of Virginia. It was a mind blowing experience for our community to spend intimate time with each other on two chartered busses from Charlottesville, VA to Appomatix, VA to Danville, VA to Greensboro, NC, to Atlanta, Ga, to Birmingham, AL, to walking across the Edmund Pettus Bridge in Selma, AL to Montgomery, AL to the Equal Justice Initiative Center with brother Bryan Stevenson (yes, the same Brian Stevenson who gave me the courage to even go forward with this).

I look at the activist attending the Albemarle County Board of Supervisors meetings and the Albemarle County School Board meetings demanding policy

239

changes, and I see an awakening. I see the collaboration between groups and populations throughout the city who are willing to be present, speak up, and simply do their part, and I feel proud. I look at the young brothers from the community like Robert Grey and Jamar Pierre Louis who are hosting annual back to school bashes with hundreds of people attending and being blessed and I see improvement.

None of these things have happened overnight.

Not all of these things have required me to be involved. All of these things came together as the community decided to heal itself opposed to sit on their hands and complain. This is the change that we can believe in. This is how a community turns a tragedy into triumph.

To date, the statue of Robert E. Lee and Stonewall Jackson is still in legal limbo. We, the city, have gone to court with the individuals for nearly a year about whether or not the statue can legally be removed from our public park. What will happen with it has yet to be determined as undoubtedly there will be decisions by judges rendered and subsequently appealed. Nonetheless, the progress that has been made occurred in spite of a tribute to a slave master who fought diligently to maintain slavery, and

240

subsequently even advocated for statues dedicated to himself not be erected. The New Charlottesville still has a long way to go. We are not removed from health and income disparities. We are not removed from gentrification or covert/overt racism. In some cases, we have seen those who oppose our efforts to become more equitable double down on their decision to undermine our community. The local chapters of the sons and daughters of the confederacy have erected a new 100-foot flag on highway I-64 about 15 miles outside of the city to send a message to our community. They even said that the flag was put it partly because of me. I wear that, just like the other foolishness as a badge of honor. This fight isn't one about a statue. It isn't one about a flag. It's about a shift in ideology. It's about a push to change a narrative. It's about an awakening. It's about a community standing up for themselves.

When we look back 10, 30, or 100 years from now on this moment in history what will be said? My hope is that it is proven that Charlottesville decided to say the ways of yesteryear would no longer be tolerated. We decided that we would stand up for what's right, even if it meant standing alone. We decided to do what was right even if it meant that a whole lot of people had to become uncomfortable.

241

This moment in history will be just that, a moment in history. My grandmother would always say that you can't get to the clear and clean water without going through a little bit of mud.

Hopefully the moments after will continue to lead us down the path to clear water.

Made in the USA
Columbia, SC
16 February 2020